One Year and Counting

One Year & Counting

Breast Cancer, My World, and Me

Susan Nethery

BAKER BOOK HOUSE
Grand Rapids, Michigan

The following publishers have given permission to use quotations from their copyrighted material:

The American Cancer Society: *Breast Cancer Fact Sheet* and *Cancer News*.

Harcourt Brace Jovanovich, Inc.: *Breast Cancer: A Personal History and An Investigative Report* by Rose Kushner, © 1975.

Mrs. Terese Lasser and Simon and Schuster: *Reach to Recovery* by Terese Lasser and William K. Clarke, © 1972.

The Macmillan Company: *What Women Should Know About the Breast Cancer Controversy* by George Crile, Jr., © 1973.

Quadrangle Books: *You Can Fight Cancer and Win* by Jane Brody, © 1976.

Real People Press: *Notes to Myself* by Hugh Prather, © 1970.

TO PAPA

who has watched helplessly as three women he loved—
his mother, his wife, and his daughter—
were stricken by cancer

Grateful Acknowledgments

. . . to Jim, whose consistent, unselfish cooperation enabled me to "find the time" to write.

. . . to Ross, Laura, Rick, and Lana, who shared their mother with a typewriter for a few months.

. . . to Bernice, who said, "Why don't you write a book?" and then cooked meals so I could "work another hour," babysat frequently, and offered invaluable help with proofreading and making copies.

. . . to Pat, who spent part of her summer vacation typing the final manuscript.

Remembering mine affliction and my misery,
The wormwood and the gall.
My soul hath them still in remembrance,
And is humbled in me.
This I recall to my mind,
Therefore have I hope!
It is of the Lord's mercies that we are not consumed,
Because his compassions fail not.
They are new every morning:
Great is thy faithfulness.

Lamentations 3:19-23

Foreword

Mastectomy must head the list of those procedures surgeons would like never to do again. The physical, mental, and emotional trauma a patient undergoes as she wakes from the anesthetic following this major surgery to find that she not only has cancer, but has had a mastectomy as well, is of such magnitude that it is difficult to put into words.

Susan Nethery is fortunate to have an intelligent, understanding, and loving husband, a close family, and praying caring friends. More important, however, is her faith and trust in God, and her knowledge of the Scriptures acquired from her Christian home, her church, and her personal studies.

Her book is the story of how a normal, healthy, young-and-attractive woman faced the crises of breast cancer and subsequent mastectomies, and at the same time developed a closer relationship to God.

The reader looking for a detailed account of a woman's problems and her reaction to them may be puzzled by Susan's frequent references to God, and may label her as some type of religious kook. Religious, yes—but if her relationship with God had consisted only of the thin, external veneer of church attendance, this would have crumbled early in her illness, leaving her without the help God continually supplied to solve her problems. Kook, yes—but Susan's sense of humor was part of that sensitivity and wisdom which kept her emotionally healthy throughout the ordeal. Susan is definitely *not* a "religious kook" in the way it is usually defined today.

Susan's reliance on God was a major part of her successful recovery and adjustment, yet her faith does not overshadow the fact that she is a woman. Having known Susan for over six years, I can assure you she has the same feelings, likes and dislikes, ideals, goals, and dreams of other young women. She has shared with me the same doubts and fears that other women experience after mastectomies. She has had to face the same problems, make the same adjustments, and restructure her lifestyle in the same ways.

Susan's book is medically accurate and informative, yet it is not textbook-type reading. The story is intensely personal, and the primary reason for the book is Susan's desire to help others. As you read her story, remember that the same God who helped her stands ready to help each of us if we will only let Him.

R. I. Garrett, M.D., F.A.C.S.
General Surgeon
Lufkin, Texas

Contents

Chapter One

About 54 million Americans now living will eventually have cancer. At present rates, one out of every 13 American women will develop breast cancer, the type cancer most frequently found in females and the leading cause of death.

Shreveport *Times* Special Supplement
Charles Sammons Cancer Center

Blessed to us is the night, for it reveals the stars.

Anonymous

Call upon me in the day of trouble:
I will deliver thee,
and thou shalt glorify me.

Psalm 50:15

On the night of May 3, 1976, several things were troubling me, but breast cancer was certainly not one of them. *That* possibility didn't enter my head at all—at least not until the next morning!

As Jim lay sleeping beside me, I tossed and turned, too much on my mind causing too much tension to allow me to relax and get the sleep I badly needed. As usual, Jim had fallen asleep quickly and easily. I've always envied him that ability. Many times I've begged for his "secret" and complained, "It's just not *fair*! Why can't I do that?"

However, with a house full of children and their constant chatter and demands, I found bedtime the only time of day for thoughts of my own and the only time quiet enough to hear myself think or listen to the "still small Voice" whose guidance I needed so desperately. All serious problems were shelved neatly in a compartment of my mind marked "Bedtime" and brought out carefully to be examined by God and me when everyone else was sleeping.

Tonight the problem was a recurrent and increasingly insistent one that soared like a giant albatross, seeming to loom even larger over me than "The Shadow of His Wings." The problem was my health.

For months now I had not been feeling well, but since the beginning of the new year the situation had definitely worsened. I agreed with Jim and my family about the probable cause, the events of the past two years in our lives were enough to get anybody down, even someone as healthy and active as I had always been.

In spite of the fact that I had ample reason to be completely run-down, I clearly realized that I could not continue to ignore the warnings that something was wrong. It was not fair to myself or my family. The past weekend had brought a new awareness of the problem to me, as all six of us had gone to Diboll, our hometown for the previous ten years before moving "back home" last July.

My sister Jeannie had invited us for the weekend, and we had looked forward eagerly to a weekend out and the chance to be with her family and old friends and to attend the church we were a part of for so long. But what should have been an enjoyable, restful vacation for me was anything but that. My head hurt constantly, I had diarrhea, I couldn't sleep, I was miserable. And for the first time I was able to admit that perhaps I should see a doctor.

Feeling the need to share my burden, I talked with Jeannie about my physical problems. I told her that I had not been to see Dr. Connell, my gynecologist in nearby Lufkin, but I had been to see our family doctor several times since the first of the year. I confided that I thought I had just worn myself out. Then I added realistically, "We just can't afford any more bills of any kind right now. And besides, *surely* if I can just get rested up, everything will be fine. After all," I said confidently, "the worst has got to be behind us now. We have survived Jim's drastic salary cut; we're in our new home; the babies' adoption papers are in our hands, and it looks like clear sailing. All I need is a little time to recuperate."

Now, back home again in my own bed, in the beautiful stillness of the night, I lay quietly savoring my favorite time of the day. Everyone was asleep; all my chores were done until tomorrow; and

I could pray, and think, and "regroup my forces" for the busy day that always came "tomorrow." I knew I was foolish to put off getting a thorough checkup. I could pray all I wanted to—"Please, dear Lord, help me feel better. I have so much to do. The house is so big. The kids need me so much. . . ." Yet I knew that although God heard my prayers, and I knew He cared, that knowledge did not relieve me of the responsibility of using the good sense He had blessed me with. I needed to see a doctor. That was that!

Having made up my mind, I nudged Jim with my elbow, wanting to discuss it with him. "Honey," I said quietly, "I'm going to call tomorrow and make an appointment to see Dr. Connell. After all, I should have gone last month anyway for my six-month breast check."

"What? You mean you missed the appointment?" Wide awake now, he propped up on one elbow and looked at me. "That was stupid," he said matter of factly.

"Now, Jim," I reasoned. "You know it's just been six months since my last xerogram and breast check. I check every month myself, you know, and there's nothing there but the usual assortment of lumps and bumps. I just couldn't see driving all the way to Lufkin and paying Dr. Connell to tell me what I already knew."

Not even bothering to answer my ridiculous argument, Jim turned back over. "Call *tomorrow*," he said with finality. And he promptly fell asleep!

Drowsy with the relief of having made a definite decision, I soon fell asleep too. My rest that night was peaceful; I had absolutely no premonition of what tomorrow would bring.

Chapter Two

95% of all breast cancers are found by women themselves.

Cancer Information Service
M.D. Anderson Hospital and Tumor Institute

Sign in Dr. Connell's office:
"If you are afraid,
you believe more in evil than you do in God."

Since the Lord is directing our steps,
why try to understand everything that happens along the way?
Proverbs 20:24 LB

I awakened the next morning to find Jim's side of the bed empty. *Boy*, I thought, *I must have been dead to the world to have missed the alarm*. Sleepily I turned toward the window to check on the day. Beautiful! A perfect May morning, and a special one, too. Today was our fourteenth anniversary! As I gazed out the large window of our second-story bedroom, I smiled contentedly. Whoever would have thought fourteen years ago that we'd be back where we started, living in our dream home in the beautiful woods of "Cat Holler" that we loved so much.

I thought again of how happy Jim's grandparents would be if they could see us now: our new home perched on the hill just to the right of where theirs used to be, our chickens in their old hen house, the smokehouse a perfect playhouse for the children. Nano died before she even saw our firstborn, but she was the one who began our dream. "Someday you children will be moving back here. Better plant some trees!" We didn't plant the trees—the future looks so far away when you're young—but we held to the dream and made it come true. And sometimes I can feel Nano's smile, beaming straight from heaven to cheer my heart.

Intruding on my quiet thoughts, like an unwelcome visitor, was the remembrance of what I must do today. What a bother! Then the thought crossed my mind: first thing Dr. Connell will say as she begins to examine me will be, "Have you noticed any changes in your breasts? Almost unconsciously, remembering it had been a little over a month since I had checked them, I began examining my right breast. "Just the usual lumpy mess," I remarked disgustedly to myself. "Who could tell if there was a real lump?"

Since Dr. Connell had discovered the first lump during a routine yearly checkup three years ago, I had been hospitalized twice and biopsied. The results were benign and diagnosed as fibro-cystic tumors, non-malignant but decidedly troublesome. As a result, I had yearly xerograms and twice-yearly breast examinations. And I religiously practiced monthly breast checks myself. After the initial panic of the first lump and surgery, I gradually began to relax. However, I presumed there was some danger of my developing cancer or they wouldn't be keeping tabs on me so carefully.

As my hand moved halfheartedly to my left breast and slowly began circling as I'd been taught, I experienced without warning that choking, panicky fright that I felt when the first lump was found three years ago. For my fingers had stopped as if paralyzed on a lump at least an inch long and very hard. *O dear God*, I thought. *This one is different. Is this what cancer feels like?*

I quickly pulled the covers up and fought to control the fear that swept over me. I heard Jim coming up the stairs, quietly singing, "This is our fourteenth anniversary, . . . the time went fast. . . ." As he appeared beside me with a cup of coffee and a kiss, I finished the phrase, a little off-key, "But with every kiss I know, I know . . . it won't be the last."

That little song, so popular during our courting days, was one we sang each anniversary, changing only the year to make it appropriate. But now I thought, *Will this be the last?*

Almost without conscious thought I made the decision not to tell Jim about the lump. Not yet. Not till after I'd talked to Dr. Connell and gotten her opinion. So we drank our coffee and made plans to go out for dinner if we could get one of the grandmothers to watch the kids.

Jim left a little before seven—he had a forty-mile school bus run to make each morning—and I got up to wake the two "big kids," Ross, who was twelve, and Laura, ten. I can't remember fixing breakfast or lunch boxes. All I could think of was calling the doctor. I knew I couldn't call before nine. Thinking back, remembering my fear, I wonder that I didn't call her at home. But I didn't even think of it! I planned to call her office, talk to Karen, her receptionist, and make an appointment—all in the usual, well-established way.

Somehow I got Ross and Laura off to school and even managed to feed and dress Rick and Lana. I was amazed and proud of my ability to function normally when I *knew* I was going to drop dead any minute from cancer. Rick, a beautiful brown-eyed boy of three, and Lana, a year-old "angel" with her curly golden hair and big blue eyes, would not even remember me! (Isn't it strange how, when you're frightened, you automatically build the worst case?—or am I the only one who does that?) After the anguish we went through to adopt those two, they wouldn't even *remember* me!

Finally, nine o'clock came, and I direct-dialed the number in Lufkin. It was busy. Impatiently I dialed again. Still busy. I put the phone down, none too gently, and walked to the other side of the kitchen.

"The Lord is my shepherd," I mumbled, trying to calm myself. "The Lord is my shepherd . . . the Lord is my shepherd. . . .

What on earth comes next?" My mind was a blank. Oh, yeah! "I shall not want." What I *want* is to get this call through!

Dialing again, I heard the welcome sound of the office phone ringing, and almost immediately Karen's familiar voice saying, "Dr. Connell's office."

"Karen, this is Susan Nethery. I've got a new lump. It's a different kind. I found it this morning, and it wasn't there a month ago, and I was going to call anyway today to make an appointment for a checkup because I haven't been feeling good for months now and. . . ."

"Wait a minute," Karen interrupted. "Dr. Connell's not even here! She won't be back in the office for two weeks."

"But listen," she said helpfully, "if it's a lump you know she'd tell you to go see Dr. Garrett. Why don't you call for an appointment with him?" She wished me well; I hung up the phone and found Dr. Garrett's number.

When the first lump was discovered, Dr. Connell had said I must see a surgeon and had rattled off the names of three who practiced in the Lufkin areas. In my state of stupor only one rang a bell. "Dr. Garrett? Is he the one whose father is a Baptist preacher?" After being assured that he was, I commented that I had seen him once at a revival service where I was playing the piano in a church his father pastored. "I'll see him, I guess. I like his daddy."

Now, as I called his office, I remembered that day with amusement. What a way to pick a surgeon! But I had never regretted my choice. He was a fine surgeon, a thoughtful, caring doctor, and a dedicated Christian. And his being Baptist was "icing on the cake!" Mary, his receptionist, and a good friend from many previous office visits, answered the phone promptly.

After I'd told her my problem, she said, "You're worried about this one, aren't you?"

"How'd you guess?" I asked wryly.

"No special reason," she laughed. "You just sound as if someone's got a gun to your back. Want to come in this afternoon? About 1:30?"

As I replaced the receiver, I thought: "What a way to spend an anniversary! There goes the lemon meringue pie I'd planned to make for Jim. Jim! I've got to call him. I've got to get a babysitter. Oh, trouble and woe!"

Why me, Lord? I joked. (Or was I joking?) *Wait just a few more minutes, Lord, and I can sit down and we'll talk about this. Just let me get everything arranged. Just help me think of a Bible verse to calm me. Peace be still, Lord? But you said that to calm a storm!*

But, yes, this is also a storm, and soon the rain will start, I thought, trying to hold back my tears till I had time to sit down and cry.

You're right. This is definitely a storm, Lord. And I'm sure glad You're in my boat.

Chapter Three

Not all lumps are cancerous; in fact, 65-80% of
breast biopsies are benign.

Breast Cancer Fact Sheet
National Cancer Institute

Life is a grindstone,
and whether it grinds a man down
or polishes him up
depends upon the stuff he is made of.

Edmond H. Babbitt

Trust in the Lord with all thine heart;
and lean not unto thine own understanding.
In all thy ways acknowledge him,
and he shall direct thy paths.

Proverbs 3:5, 6

Exhausted, I curled up in the corner of the car and rested my head on the seat. Less than three hours had passed since I made my appointment with Dr. Garrett, but those few hours had been crammed with frantic activity. I had called Jim, and he had offered to drive me to Lufkin "since it was our anniversary." He had been calm and unruffled, as he normally is, and his calmness had its usual steadying effect on me. Now, as we drove along in the bright May sunshine, his presence was just the comfort I needed.

I am so blessed, I thought, *to have a loving heavenly Father and a husband like Jim.* Now that I had talked to each of them, I was no longer alone with my problem. The burden was being shared, and I was relieved, relaxed, and ready to face whatever came.

For most of the hour it took to make the trip we drove in silence, each thinking his own thoughts, our hands and hearts touching reassuringly. I had already explained about the lump; we knew the children were happy and well-cared-for with Jim's mother, and we were both gratefully aware that God was in control of our situation. So there was really not much to say except to make small talk, and neither of us was in the mood for that. All I really remember discussing was where we would eat our anniversary dinner!

I had dressed with care this morning, not only because of the trip to the doctor's office, but because of our planned dinner. I had found the time to wash and blow-dry my reddish-blond hair, which was cut very short. I had on a new dress I had made and worn for the first time to church several weeks ago. I remember thinking I looked like an Easter egg! The ripe-watermelon color of the dress, with its brilliant splashes of sunflower yellow and lavender, and my yellow shoes and earrings to match made me a riot of color. I had chosen that particular dress because of its cheerfulness. And because it was easy and quick to get into and out of! How surprised I'd have been to know that even *that* dress would be extremely difficult to get on and off in a few months.

Typically female, I felt better when I knew I looked good. The lump in my breast didn't seem so earth-shatteringly important now that I was all dressed up, going *out*, actually, for dinner, with the kids and the housework a "million" miles behind me. This may be a good day after all, I mused. Who am I to say a lump is *cancer* just because it *feels* different? Experienced doctors can't even diagnose by feel alone. This is all going to turn out to be my imagination, and I'm going to feel pretty foolish. But I sure will be happy, too!

This welcome quiet time gave me a chance to reflect on God's goodness to me. Counting my blessings was an exercise which never failed to lift my spirits. As I expressed my thanks today, I added an apology to God for my fear and for reacting to a frightening situation as a mere mortal without the supernatural strength of the Almighty God at my disposal. Once again I thanked Him for His Son Jesus, who had *been* here, in human shoes (or sandals!), and understood what a *burden* it was sometimes to be human.

Thank You, dear Father, that even in my fear I knew You were nearby. Thank You for Your Holy Spirit within me that prompted me, even in near panic, to remember the source of peace and calm in every situation. Thank You for another opportunity to grow, even though I can't see how I can humanly stand any more of the molding and shaping that precedes growth right now. I'm so tired, Father. You know what all our family has been through lately. Do You honestly think it's time for another lesson? What if I fail You again, as I have so often, just when I've come to depend on You more than I ever have in my life? I'm so ashamed, You know, each time I goof, to get back up and face You, especially when You so generously offer a chance to take one giant step forward after I've stumbled backwards three. Too often, as You well know, I strike out eagerly on my own and forget to say, Father, may I?

Knowing that the memory of God's help in the past gives strength for present crises, I tried to recall briefly the events of the previous two years. I thought of how Jim and I had faced more trouble than we'd ever known and yet had been blessed and helped, sometimes miraculously, beyond all expectation.

*   *   *

We were so content and happy, our little family of four, when worlds of unexpected trouble arrived in the form of two adorable babies. Many stories have been told of "babies left on doorsteps," but this is almost literally what happened to us.

We had already decided to limit our children to the two beautiful, healthy, normal ones we had. In fact, we had taken irrevocable steps to insure that fact. But God had other plans for us, and in the summer of 1974 he added two new members to our family—Rick, who was then nineteen months old, and two months later his newborn sister, Lana.

Ours was a classic story of a mother (whom we had not known before) giving up her children "for their own good" and then, months later, changing her mind. We knew we could not allow these two babies, whom we loved dearly already, to go back into the situation they came from. (This cannot be discussed here, although I wish it could, lest some would think us heartless in trying to take children from their parents. However, *we* know, and *God* knows, and our hearts are perfectly at peace.)

We decided, after much prayer and deep thought, to do everything we could to insure these children a chance for a normal, healthy, loved-and-cared-for life. It was a decision that was to change our lives.

A year and a half was to go by before the children were legally ours. Those years were anguish for me, involving court battles, lawyers, the Child Welfare Department, and visits for the children with their natural parents until the welfare people succeeded in getting termination of parental rights. It seemed an eternity before we were eventually able to adopt the children.

So many people were helpful and supportive to us during this time, and God gave us the strength to go through with it; but even now, to think about what I went through, as a "mother" of two children who might be taken from me, is almost more than I can bear.

Many people wondered why we would take on a problem of that magnitude and cautioned us against "trouble later" with the natural parents, "trouble later" if the children should have inherited the problems of their parents, and "trouble later" when the children grew up and wanted to know "who they were." Jim and I didn't need to be reminded of all the problems—we were aware of them. We also knew we had no choice but to try to help Rick and Lana. However you may privately anguish over the cruelties and injustices many people of the world face, you cannot help them all. But what excuse can you give to yourself, and how can you live with yourself, if you don't help the ones you *can*?

We knew one other thing: God brought them to us; therefore, He would help us. And He did!

In our desire to protect our two new children, and ourselves, we began to seriously consider making the big move back home. It was something we had always planned to do anyway, eventually, and now seemed a propitious time to try. Jim began looking for a job in the area and almost immediately found an opening in the Hemphill school system. (*Thank You, Lord!*) However, the job was as tax assessor-collector, an unpopular job to say the least! (*Well, Lord, Matthew was a tax collector—they're not all bad!*) And Jim would have to drive a school bus in addition to his job to make even a livable salary for our big family. The new job would entail a severe cut in salary from his present job as accountant in Diboll. (*Lord, You promised to supply our needs—looks like we'll be putting You to the test!*)

After weighing all the pros and cons and praying for direction, we decided to make the move. We sold our home for a considerable profit, got a loan for the additional money we felt we needed to build our new home, and jumped in with all four feet. In June of 1975 we moved to our new location, into the only house available for occupancy: an old two-bedroom frame house, with a bathroom that didn't work because the well stayed dry all summer (and the commode wouldn't flush when it *wasn't* dry), no hot water at all (and seldom any cold), nothing to cook on but a hot plate and an electric skillet, no airconditioning or heat, and no washer or dryer.

That was a chapter in my life that was trying, to say the least. The majority of the problems stemming from that period of time could have been avoided if we'd moved in with either of our parents, both of whom invited us and would have welcomed us.

But Jim and I adamantly refused to consider it because we felt it would be unwise.

At first living in the small house was fun—a summer-long campout ahead! But it didn't take long for it to get old, especially for me. It was really difficult to care for four kids, two of them babies, with no running water. Preparing meals was a major job and cleaning up worse, and the mountains of laundry had to be transported to my mother's house or Jim's mother's and then brought back "home" to hang out on the line to dry. (I did have a clothesline!)

I had never fully realized my strength as a woman before that summer. It actually became a challenge to make a pleasant home out of our little house, and I came to realize that, although I would not *choose* to stay there, if I knew *I had* to I could make it. It was a valuable lesson.

The summer-long campout stretched into fall; it was Thanksgiving week before we finally moved into our new home. During all those months, I had also been working every spare minute, literally, at the building site of our new home. *All* of us worked—both my family and Jim's. My mom and my mother-in-law fixed most of our evening meals, babysat (until school started—they are both teachers), and encouraged us. My mother and I cleared the land, hauling, hoeing, and burning so that the men could be free to work inside. In addition, we did all the cleaning up after the carpenters—sweeping mountains of sawdust and debris—so that we wouldn't have to pay them for doing what we could do ourselves.

The men—Jim, my daddy, his daddy, even neighbors, brothers, friends—did absolutely all the work they could possibly do themselves. There is no way to measure all we owe to others for our new house; it truly represents a labor of love.

But, to look at the bright side, I have expanded my capabilities to include the wallpaper hanging, sanding, sealing, and staining woodwork and cabinets, putting in insulation, and floating out sheetrock! In addition I decorated the house, made myriads of decisions (that in itself can drive you batty) and shopped for months—relentlessly, doggedly, searching for the best prices on everything.

Looking back, I cannot see anything that we could have done differently to make it easier. We had four excellent carpenters, but we had to do as much as we could ourselves because of financial problems. We could have built a smaller house and gotten a turn-key job, but we were building for a lifetime, and we have a large family. We cut corners where we could, but some things we definitely wanted. We were willing to work for them, and work we did!

Personally I drove myself to the limits of my strength. I don't even know now how I did what I did, but I remember I prayed a lot, and I cried a lot—and I just kept going because I didn't have a choice. Later that training was to prove invaluable. Sometimes you have to do things, even beyond what you *can* do, *because you have no choice.*

I learned another valuable lesson: unless you really put your heart and soul into a project and then see it completed, you cannot know the supreme sense of accomplishment when that dream becomes a reality. Moving into our lovely new home was one of the happiest days of our lives. We had put ourselves into that house, and although the mortgage wasn't paid, we knew it was ours in the real sense of the word.

Two passages of Scripture came to mind as I thought of

building the house. Both of them I had copied and placed in my Bible so I could readily find them. When everything was going wrong, and we actually began to wonder if perhaps we had not heard the Lord right when He indicated moving, I found the following:

> Even though the fig trees are all destroyed,
> and there is neither blossom left nor fruit,
> and though the olive crops all fail,
> and the fields lie barren;
> even if the flocks die in the fields
> and the cattle barns are empty,
> *Yet I Will Rejoice in the Lord;*
> I will be happy in the God of my salvation.

Habakkuk 3:17-18 LB

And later, as I went from door to door in my own private dedication of this house to God, I prayed on each threshold: *Protect us, O God, in our new home. Guard us from the Evil One. Keep hatred, uncleanness, unbelief, and all things displeasing to You from entering here. I welcome You in to make Your abode with us.*

And then I read aloud the following prayer (adapted from Psalm 144:12-15):

> *Help us, our Father,*
> That our sons may be as plants grown up in their youth;
> That our daughters may be as corner stones, polished after the similitude of a palace;
> That our garners may be full, affording all manner of store;
> That our sheep may bring forth thousands and ten thousands in our streets;
> That our oxen may be strong to labour;
> That there be no breaking in, nor going out;

That there be no complaining in our streets.
Happy is that people, that is in such a case:
Yea, happy is that people, whose God is the Lord.

Now, six months later, our pleasure in our new home had been dimmed only by my seeming inability to regain my strength. Yet remembering, as I was this morning, the staggering physical and mental strain of the past few years, I became certain that my problem was purely one of fatigue. I had just overdone it and this was my body's only way of saying, "Enough!"

Soon we would be in Lufkin; Dr. Garrett could give me some vitamins and something to help my stomach, assure me that this was just another fibro-cystic lump, and send me home with a stern admonishment to get some rest.

Convinced now that I had just been shaken up this morning so that I would realize I had to take better care of myself, and confident that I'd be better even by tomorrow, I turned to Jim and said daringly: "El Chico's! Let's eat *Mexican* food! I feel like celebrating and paying for it tomorrow!"

Chapter Four

Aspirating the fluid from a cyst almost always cures it permanently. Cancers, of course, almost never contain fluid, so if a cyst is aspirated and there is no longer any lump, there is no danger of cancer.
What Women Should Know About the Breast Cancer Controversy
George Crile, Jr., M.D.

If I keep a green bough in my heart,
The singing bird will come.
Chinese Saying

And we know that all things work together for good
to them that love God,
to them who are the called according to his purpose.
Romans 8:28

Ordinarily I didn't have to wait long to see Dr. Garrett, and today was no exception. I appreciated the fact that he didn't crowd his schedule with too many appointments, because I could generally count on seeing him at my appointed time.

It had been three years since I'd been here. My last surgery had been in January of 1973, and except for a few months of post-operative care, that had been my last contact with him. I found myself looking forward to renewing what had been a pleasant relationship. I was comfortable with him and didn't hesitate to say what I felt or thought; in return, he was a concerned listener and adviser, and as far as I knew he had always been honest with me.

Jim and I glanced through magazines and chatted with Mary until Dr. Garrett came to the door and called for me. His greeting was pleasant. "Haven't seen you in a long time. No trouble, is there?"

He escorted me into the examining room. "Just a lump I found this morning. It feels different . . . more defined, firmer than the usual 'tough oatmeal' stuff."

"You get undressed and we'll check it out." He walked into his office, and Mary and I talked as I stripped to the waist and got settled on the examining table. Her foot on the pedal that raised the table was, I assumed, the signal to Dr. Garrett that I was "presentable" and ready. Immediately he came in and, making small talk, began to examine me.

"The lump is right—" I began, but was interrupted.

"Wait. Let me see if I can find it."

As his hands checked my right breast and armpit expertly, I waited impatiently. Finally he began on the armpit and outside of the left one. (Later I learned that most cancerous lumps are located in the upper outer quadrant of the breast near the armpit.)

"You sure are lumpy," he commented, unconcernedly.

Soon his fingers reached the inner, upper quadrant where The Lump was located. I held my breath. What if he didn't feel anything? What if I were making a gigantic fool of myself?

But his fingers stopped, probing gently all over and around the lump. Absurdly relieved, I resumed breathing.

"That's a lump all right."

"And that's a profound medical diagnosis if I ever heard one," I observed dryly. "Now, what is it?"

"Just a fluid-filled cyst, I think. I'm going to draw the fluid out with a needle."

"You can say 'aspirate'; I know what it means. I may be lumpy but I'm not a dummy." I enjoyed the light bantering that usually went on between us; it relieved the tension today and was one of the reasons I felt so comfortable with him.

"Well, if you know so much, you know it's going to hurt a little bit—about like getting a shot."

Meanwhile, Mary had prepared the needle and cleaned the area around the lump with alcohol. Trying to hold the lump firmly between the fingers of his left hand, Dr. Garrett jabbed the needle into the hard tissue. From *my* point of reference, it felt like the needle was trying to penetrate a bone. It also hurt. I was glad when he withdrew the needle.

"Well? Did you get it?"

"Must've missed it." (I knew he hadn't. A little bell of alarm rang clearly in my head.) "I'm going to try again. Hold still one more time." Again the pain of insertion, the needle meeting with resistance, the needle withdrawn. Again, no fluid!

"Well, it's not a fluid-filled cyst, but that's all it means. I'm certain it is a fibro-cystic tumor, but the only way to be sure is to biopsy" (surgical removal of a sample of the suspicious breast tissue to be examined under a microscope for cancer cells).

Full of questions, I began, "But what is your *opinion*—?" Again I was interrupted. "Get your clothes on and come on into the office. We'll talk about it there."

A few minutes later, seated comfortably in front of his desk, I asked again, "What do you think? Does it feel *bad* to you?"

"It feels like a lump. You know I always recommend removing any lumps. When do you want to go into the hospital?"

Stalling for a few minutes' time to think I told him about my other problems, about our move to the country, our adopting two kids, and the strain I'd been under. After I had rehearsed my symptoms in detail, he suggested that I check into the hospital a few days before surgery and have some tests run. "Give you a chance to get a few days' rest, too. Sounds like it might possibly be gall bladder trouble, but we can check that out."

"I can't possibly come in before school is out. My babysitters are both school teachers. The week after school is out would really be better for all of us. Jim can take his vacation then.

"That'll be fine. There's no rush. Just call Mary and tell her when you decide for sure, and we'll fix you up. Meanwhile, lay off the coffee and cokes and the fried and spicy foods. You might try an antacid after each meal and a glass of milk at bedtime. And try to get a little rest."

With nothing in his manner or speech to cause me any alarm, I felt quite relieved. If he thought this was *cancer*, he'd have me in the hospital in a hurry, wouldn't he?

"Don't worry," he said. "You're too young for breast cancer! See you in the hospital in a few weeks."

*   *   *

"Goodness knows I don't want to go to the hospital again," I mumbled through a mouthful of tortilla chips, "but I *still* feel uneasy about this lump. If it *is* cancer, which it *can't* be, it seems to me waiting a few weeks isn't a good idea."

Sitting in the red-upholstered booth of the restaurant, stuffing ourselves on the infrequent treat of Mexican food, we had tried, unsuccessfully, to change our topic of conversation from lumps, bumps, and hospital bills to a more cheerful discourse. We might as well have tried to fly.

"But *you're* the one who told the doctor you couldn't possibly go before then. You know we can manage something." Jim was a little worried, too, but he was very adept at hiding his concern from me. Yet I was trying to feel him out and get him to make a definite statement. In fact, I wanted him to *tell* me what to do. He couldn't, of course, because he didn't know any more about it than I did.

Although we knew the children were fine for the rest of the evening, and our folks expected us to stay in Lufkin to celebrate our anniversary, somehow we just wanted to get home.

Late that night, after all the children were in bed, I took a long, hot bath and reviewed the day in my mind. I realized that, although I was no longer *afraid*, I was still just as certain that the lump was cancer. Under my soapy fingers, it was very pronounced, though not visible. I couldn't keep my hands away from it, unrealistically hoping that the *next* time I felt it, it would be gone. Or at least not be *cancer*.

I made a decision there in the bathtub that May night to follow the advice my mother gave when she heard our report of the day: "Why don't you go to Dr. Winslow and see what he says? I know he's just a G.P., but he has always given our family good advice and care. See what he thinks about the lump and if he thinks it is safe to wait."

She's right, I thought. *Another opinion certainly won't hurt, and I can't see Dr. Connell for several weeks. I don't blame Dr. Garrett for not being overly concerned. He knows my history of benign breast disease; he knows I'm not in any high-risk age group; I can't expect him to get all excited over a woman's intuition. He probably doesn't even believe in it.*

*   *   *

Two days later I was again lying on an examining table—this time in Dr. Winslow's office. He had just given me the most thorough breast check I'd ever had. I had been turned every way but upside down; I had clasped my hands in front of me and pulled; I had stretched my arms up over my head.

He must not have anything else to do today, I decided, as the examination dragged on. *Or else he really knows what he's doing.* I hoped it was the latter, because I certainly had better things to do. And this was not my idea of fun.

He adjusted the paper sheet to cover me, stepped back two paces, and pointed his finger in my face. "That lump has got to come out immediately, young lady. I think it's cancer!"

Unable to speak because my heart had taken a leap up into my throat, I sat there dumbly, tears springing to my eyes. But I was not upset because I was frightened; I was teary-eyed from relief. I *wanted* to hear exactly what he had said, because it confirmed what I *knew* and gave me a needed basis for action. I truly appreciated his honesty.

"You really ought to go tomorrow. In fact I think Dr. Garrett should have put you in the hospital immediately, especially since he aspirated that lump." (It was over a year later that I learned that contrary to the opinion held by a lot of doctors, putting a needle into a cancer does not cause it to get into the bloodstream.) Continuing dramatically, Dr. Winslow encouraged me to call Dr. Garrett and tell him I wanted that thing out *now*.

I was unable to ask coherent, sensible questions, so I merely thanked him and went home. Once there, my mind began to function again. I began to think the problem through in a more rational manner.

I still did not know which doctor was right, although my personal intuition told me Dr. Winslow was. Even if I were right, and I had breast cancer, I did not know if a few weeks' wait would hurt anything. I knew it would be easier for all concerned if I could wait until school was out for the summer, but I also realized that if there was the slightest chance of metastasis during those weeks, the wait was definitely not worth the risk.

Finally, after much careful deliberation, earnest assurance from Jim and our parents that I didn't need to worry about the children, and sincere prayers for God's direction, I decided to get it over with.

A week and a half later I checked into the hospital.

Chapter Five

Perhaps the best presently available method of detecting early breast cancer is by the type of mammography known as xero-radiography. The same type of sensitized plate that is used in the Xerox-copying machine is exposed to a low dose of X ray and gives a detailed picture of the structure of the breast, showing ducts and blood vessels, and lobules of breast tissue. The tiny dots of calcium that are commonly present in cancer can be easily seen on xerograms.

What Women Should Know About the Breast Cancer Controversy
George Crile, Jr., M.D.

We are holding a light. We are to let it shine! Though it may seem but a twinkling candle in a world of blackness, it is our business to let it shine.

Billy Graham

Yea, though I walk through the valley of the shadow of death, I will fear no evil: for thou art with me; thy rod and thy staff they comfort me.

Psalm 23:4

I always think of my trip into Lufkin that May 16 Sunday with amusement, for all of Lufkin, it seemed, had turned out to welcome me! Each side of the highway around the loop was crowded with people, making, literally, a human circle around the city. "What an arrival! Just look at all the people who came out to wish me well!" I laughed as I turned to Jim. "I wonder how they all knew?"

Of course, in reality, these people were not gathered for the purpose of providing me a triumphal entry into their city. Jim and I knew that this was part of Lufkin's bicentennial celebration in this eventful year of 1976—to encircle the entire city with love and prayer. It was a beautiful thing to see, especially when we passed a group of people whom we recognized as members of the Diboll church where we had been members for so long. I waved eagerly and returned their smiles as they recognized us. Seeing them gave my spirits a special boost, for I knew that they were aware of my problem and had been praying for me.

I remember the warm feeling that flooded my heart when we were *inside* that circle of Christian love as we turned off the loop and into the hospital parking lot. That feeling remained with me throughout the day, and suddenly everything seemed funny and adventurous. I decided right then that I was going to enjoy this hospital stay, be cheerful and optimistic, and see what all I could learn that I hadn't known before. My curiosity is insatiable—it's one of the joys of life to me. There's so much I haven't seen and done and tried—and in some cases too much that I have—that I get itchy feet just thinking about it!

Jim and I laughed (quietly, behind her back) at the poor lady who admitted us and couldn't get anything right. We laughed when the nurse escorted me to my room and found Jim already there, lying on the bed watching a ball game. (He had gone on ahead to take my luggage, while I had to go by the lab for blood tests.) We laughed when an X-ray technician came to get me for a chest X-ray and couldn't find his patient. (I hadn't gotten undressed yet, and *Jim* was in the bed!)

We had a good time that evening, and if Jim was worried about anything, I didn't know it. He left about six o'clock so he could get home to put all the kids to bed. I still wasn't sure just what the plans were for all of them; everyone had said, "Just let us worry about them." But I knew Jim agreed with me that it would be best if they stayed home as much as possible. Lana was so young, and Rick, at that time, was still insecure about being away from home. He had so many emotional scars from his life before we got him that I really worried about his reaction to my leaving him.

I settled into my beautiful room with enjoyment. I was in the new women's wing, and the private room I occupied had a lively green jungle-print wall covering, a colorful bedspread, and carpet on the floor. I felt like a lady of leisure, rich and pampered, without a thing to do but lie around and read the exciting new magazines I had brought with me. I put on the thin, silky negligee Jim had bought me for our anniversary. The gown was white, with sprinkles of little pink flowers. The top was cut to a low "V" and the skirt flared gently to the floor from soft gathers under the bosom. The matching long-sleeved robe side-wrapped and tied under my breasts, and it fit as if it were made for me. Jim loved it on me, and wearing it tonight made me feel closer to him, though in reality he was already sixty miles away.

I said a special prayer for him that night. I knew that while I was up here being waited on, he was going to have a tough week. Not only did he have four children to look after, as well as his job, but he had the burden of worrying about me. I knew that the few days until my surgery on Wednesday would be interminable to him, and I was sorry for what he had to go through because of me.

As I arranged things around my bed, I put two things within close reach. My Bible was put on the nightstand beside my bed—not for show (although I hoped it *would* be a witness to someone) but because I knew that having it in plain view would be a challenge and a source of strength to me. If that Bible were there in sight of all, it would be mute testimony that I *claimed*, at least, to be a Christian. Therefore, I simply could *not* disappoint my Lord by being unkind, inconsiderate, complaining, or worried.

The other item I put at my bedside was the precious little hospital book my Laura had made for me. The front page read, "My Mother's Booklet, by your oldest daughter," and it was brightly decorated throughout with flowers, hearts, and rainbows. Inside were special little messages:

I love you, Mom,
I really do,
I hope you really love me, too.

And on another page:

When it's a gloomy day,
And I'm feeling bad in a way,

You come and tell me something fine,
         You're just like sunshine!

Also inside were pictures of "Jim Nethery, your husband," "Ross, your oldest son," "Laura, your oldest daughter," "Rick, your youngest son," and "Lana, your baby." There were several empty pages for visitors' signatures. I was delighted with the book, and it proved helpful many times later to break the tension when visitors would come and not know what to say. "Will you sign my book?" I'd ask, and, relieved at the reprieve, they'd respond eagerly and enjoy looking through it. I was often thankful for that book and especially thankful for the sweet, loving little girl who had made it.

*   *   *

The next few days passed rapidly. I was constantly going to the first-floor radiation center for one test or the other; Dr. Garrett checked on me twice a day; friends and family were always coming by. Part of my worries were soon laid to rest as Dr. Garrett reported that there was no sign of gall bladder trouble, an ulcer, or colon trouble. I was relieved, naturally, but I thought, *Yuk! All those enemas, that castor oil, drinking that liquid chalk, and those horrid upper and lower G.I. series for nothing!*

"I think all you need to do is watch your diet. Stay on a bland one for a while, and rest a little more. Tomorrow we'll get a xerogram done, and I'll let you know what time your surgery will be so you can call your family. We've got to get you out of here; you're just lying up here taking it easy when there's not a thing wrong with you!"

"You won't release me from here before you get a chance to cut on me! I know why you've got me here: you need the money to pay for that fancy new office you're building!"

With a cheery "See you tomorrow," he left the room. Immediately I called home to tell Jim the good news. He reported that all was fine there, and I urged him not to come to see me that night. "Just wait till Wednesday morning. I'll call you tomorrow to tell you what time."

Later that evening Dr. Connell came by. I was so glad to see her, and she explained that Dr. Garrett had let her office know I was here. She examined my breasts and agreed that the new lump felt different from anything I'd had previously.

"You shouldn't have missed your breast check last month, you know. However, it's been only six months since your last xerogram. If this were cancerous it would have shown up at some stage then. I'm not worried about it, but you did the right thing by going to see Dr. Garrett. I definitely think it should come out."

I accepted the reprimand for the missed appointment graciously. Yet I couldn't resist an attempt to justify my actions. "This lump was not *there* when it was time for my breast check. I don't care whether it could have or couldn't have; it did just come all of a sudden."

She wanted to know about Jim and the children; we discussed her recent trip, and my escapades of the past year. It was always pleasant talking with Dr. Connell. She was well-loved by her many patients, and one of the reasons was because it was obvious that she *cared*. She was attentive and interested and never made me feel rushed when I saw her for office visits. She had been my doctor since we moved to the area when I was almost three months pregnant with Laura. I had continued to see her, mostly for yearly checkups, ever since.

"I'll check in again tomorrow after we see the xerograms. Tell

Jim 'Hello' for me." As she left I thought how glad I was that she was back in town!

*　　*　　*

Having a xerogram made is no fun, but it's not really too unpleasant. Yet if I were an overly sensitive, extremely modest person (which I'm not), I think I would avoid having one like the plague! It just *is* a little embarrassing to lie on a cold, hard, examining table, naked from the waist up, while fully-clothed strangers peer at you, poke you, twist and turn and handle you.

"Relax. Hold perfectly still." (How can you possibly relax and be perfectly still at the same time?)

Leaving the room after painstakingly getting the breast in exactly the right position under the big white balloon, the technician peeks at you from a tiny window.

"Take a deep breath. Let it out. Take a deep breath. Hold it! Now relax."

Today's picture-taking was like any other of the several times I've had it done. *Except for one thing.* Always before, the pictures had been taken to a doctor, briefly, to see if they were clear enough. Several times retakes have had to be made. But I never saw the doctor.

Today, not only were retakes made, but the heretofore invisible doctor made an appearance. (The alarm bell in my mind jangled again.)

"I'm Dr. Shelton," said a smiling, white-coated man with a mustache. (He could have passed for Santa Claus if he'd had a white beard, just because of the twinkle in his eyes.) "The picture wasn't definite." (*Hmm*, I thought, *why not just take another?*) "Show me where this lump is." Deftly he examined my breast.

"What does it feel like?" I managed to stammer, still a little dazed from my discovery that there really *was* a doctor who studied those pretty blue pictures. (Yes, Virginia, there *is* a Santa Claus!)

"Oh, the film was a little hazy. Just wanted to check it myself. Nothing to worry about. . . ." Evasion tactics if ever I heard any! Before I had time to formulate another question, he was gone. (And giving a nod up the chimney he rose. . . .)

I was escorted back to the phone-booth-sized cubicle that served as a dressing room; shortly afterward I was wheeled back up to my room. I was indignant. I didn't know anything more *after* seeing the doctor than I had before. After all, whose breast *was* this anyway! I can't speak for all patients, but *I* want to know everything about everything that concerns *me*. I don't like secrets; I don't like surprises; I don't like being "sheltered."

If Dr. Shelton had known how exciting it would have been for me to see those X-rays—just to see what the inside of me looked like—would he have shown them to me? I doubt it. If he had known how much easier it would have been on me to have said, "Look. This lump is suspicious. There's a possibility it's malignant," instead of leaving me full of wonderings, would he have told me? I doubt it.

I didn't want a complete, positive signed-in-blood diagnosis! I just wanted to know what some of these brilliant medical minds *thought* it was. (I'm not being completely fair—I'm writing from hindsight, realizing *now* that I was not told the whole truth. *Then* I merely felt frustrated because I felt the doctors' evasiveness.)

It was after five o'clock before Dr. Garrett made his evening rounds. I was determined to get some answers.

"What did the xerogram show?"

"We can't say for sure until we get in there."

So much for my determination. I decided to be kind. I didn't want to put the poor doctor through any unnecessary stress; after all he had had a busy day, bless his little heart.

"Okay. I give up. Can you *possibly* tell me, although I realize I'm just the patient, what you will do when you get in there to whatever you happen to find?"

Evidently this was easier. He relaxed. "If the lump is like the others, you already know the procedure. I'll remove it, stitch you up, and you'll be out of here in a couple of days. If, on the other hand, it's malignant, I'll go ahead and remove the breast before you wake up."

"How long will the surgery take?" I asked calmly, as if he hadn't just said he might remove my breast tomorrow.

"About an hour for a benign tumor, about four hours otherwise."

Suddenly I could think of no more questions. *I know there is more I should ask*, I thought, panicking. *Here I am faced with possible amputation of a breast and I can't think what to ask!* There just didn't seem to be anything else to say.

"I'll think of a million things I want to ask you when you've gone, but right now there's only one more thing. What time is my surgery scheduled? I need to call Jim."

"You're first on my schedule tomorrow—probably around 7:30. I'll see you before they put you under. Sleep good."

And he was gone. Put me under? Six feet under, maybe?

Dr. Connell came by later. "Just checking on you," she said, sticking her head in the door. "Good luck in the morning."

I had several calls to make, to friends and family who wanted to know what time surgery would be, but first I had to call Jim. The phone rang and rang, and I was a little peeved that no one was there to answer it. "Guess they're all outside having a good time," I pouted.

I hung the phone up, disappointed that I couldn't talk to Jim before I called anyone else. I got up and put my robe on to go down the hall to watch the babies for awhile (a favorite pastime) before trying to call home again. Just as I reached the door it opened— and in walked Jim!

"Oh, Jim! I'm so glad to see you. What are you doing here? I just tried to call you. Where are the kids? You shouldn't have come tonight!"

But, oh, how glad I was that he had come. I walked down to the cafeteria with him to get a hamburger; we watched the babies a few minutes and enjoyed being with several people who came to see me.

About 8:30 a nurse's aide came in and ran everybody out so she could prep me. She washed my chest, my arm, my abdomen (my *abdomen?*) and proceeded to shave me in all those well-scrubbed places.

"Why are you shaving my right side?"

"That's what you do for gall bladder surgery," she replied.

"Gall bladder surgery! I'm not *having* gall bladder surgery."

"That's what your sheet says here, honey. That's my orders."

Baffled, I didn't comment further. But almost before she left room I was on the phone to Dr. Garrett. "Is there something you didn't tell me? Why was I prepped for a gall bladder surgery?"

"Oh, good grief. They've made a mistake. I put that down originally in case you needed it so I'd be allowed plenty of time in the operating room. Go to sleep and quit worrying!"

Jim stayed until the "pill nurse" made her rounds with my sleeping pill. "See you in the morning. Think you can get up that early?" he teased. And with a goodnight kiss he left and went to his brother's house. (Ken and Linda lived in Lufkin.)

I knew I needed a good night's sleep, but there was something I needed more right then. Picking up my Bible, I opened it to Psalm 23, reading the familiar verses I had read before each previous surgery. Somehow the unconscious, drugged "twilight zone" I would be in during surgery made me think of the "valley of the shadow of death," and these verses were comforting.

I prayed that night, but only briefly. Somehow I couldn't think of the right questions to ask *Him* either.

Chapter Six

Radical mastectomy is an extensive operation in which not only the breast is removed but also the overlying skin, the two big muscles of the chest wall, and all of the fatty tissue and lymph nodes in the axilla (armpit). As much as possible of the fat is removed from the skin, so that the skin is almost paper-thin and lies directly on the ribs.

What Women Should Know About the Breast Cancer Controversy
George Crile, Jr., M.D.

Reach out, O God, to touch my body with the cool hands of Thy compassion. Press to my lips the cup of Thy strength. Ease the burden of my pain, O Lord, and give me courage to endure the pain which cannot be eased. Make my mind to relax. Help me to be still and know that Thou art God.

Everett B. Lesher

Humble yourselves therefore under the mighty hand of God, that he may exalt you in due time: *Casting all your care upon him; for he careth for you.* Be sober, be vigilant; because your adversary the devil, as a roaring lion, walketh about, seeking whom he may devour: Whom resist steadfast in the faith, knowing that the same afflictions are accomplished in your brethren that are in the world.

1 Peter 5:6-9

I was awake before the nurse reached my bedside from the door. Years of being a mother had tuned my ears to pick up the slightest sounds. (Jim says I sleep *awake*!) "Susan? It's time to wake up."

I switched on the overhead light and reached for my watch. Six o'clock. I saw that the young nurse's aide (*Bonnie*, I remembered, from an early enema the day before!) had a clean towel and a hospital gown. "Good morning," I said cheerfully. "What's next?"

"You need to get up and shower and put on this *lovely* gown I've brought. You'll be getting your pre-op hypo in a little while, and we don't want you up after that. Don't drink anything," she reminded me, and I recalled that the night nurse had taken away my water pitcher the night before.

"I *have* to brush my teeth," I stated flatly.

"Okay. Just don't swallow the water. I'll be back in a little while."

It didn't take me long to shower. (If I'd known then what I knew later, I would have stayed under that delicious stream of hot water as long as possible. I had no idea how long it would be before I would enjoy that taken-for-granted pleasure again.) As I was drying off, I heard the door open. "Bonnie? I'll be right out. . . ." There was no reply.

The bathroom door handle turned slowly and I froze. "Bonnie?" I tried again.

"No, it's the big bad wolf!"

"O *Jim*, you scared me to death! What are you doing here so early?"

"I couldn't sleep." (*Jim* couldn't sleep?) "And I wanted to see you before you got your shot." He looked at me, and his eyes got misty.

"I love you," he said simply.

I dropped the towel and flung my arms around his neck, overcome by the emotion of the moment. Tears ran down my cheeks as I clung to him. "I love you, too. And I'm scared. What if . . . what if I . . . what if it's. . . ." I stammered to a halt and started over. "What if they cut off my breast?"

As usual Jim saved the day. "So?" he quipped, in his best fake southern drawl, "It ain't no big thing!"

"Oh, *you!*" I shrieked, laughing through my tears. "That's the way you talk about an old friend?" I laughed again remembering something Jim had said a couple of weeks ago. . . .

He had come into the kitchen where I was fixing supper, a worried look on his face. Sensing a serious conversation, I turned to face him. "About that lump you found. . . ."

"Yes?" I replied solemnly.

Poker-faced, he continued. "Are you sure it wasn't your *breast?*"

Grateful for the laughter, and for Jim, I recovered my mental equilibrium and the towel at about the same time.

"Now if you don't get out of here I'm going to pull this emergency cord. And when sixteen nurses come charging in here I'm going to cry 'Rape!' and see what happens to you!"

"And Jim," I grabbed his arm as he went out, serious again. "Don't tell Mama and Papa I cried."

*   *   *

About six-thirty Jim opened the door to admit Mother and Daddy, his mother and father, and Ross and Laura. We had both decided that the kids should be there. They were old enough to be included in this important family affair. Later I discovered that these six were just the first of many who waited anxiously for the outcome of my surgery in the tiny seventh floor waiting room.

"Goodness!" I greeted them. "Did they close the school down today? Can't see how they can open the doors without all of you!" (My mama taught fifth grade, Papa taught in high school, and Bernice, my mother-in-law, was librarian.)

We were interrupted by a green-clad nurse who said she would be taking care of me in the recovery room. "When I ask you to," she instructed, "I want you to take deep breaths for me. It'll help you wake up."

"I will if I can remember," I laughed, thinking that sounded like a strange request. (*Is this hypnosis? Am I being programmed?*)

"You'll remember," she said confidently, and she left.

Everyone seemed in good spirits. We were all trying to let each other know how unconcerned we were, I think! This was not a sham, but an act of love. We all knew, to some extent, the gravity of the situation; yet each wanted to bear the burden for the others. I knew that any one of the people in that room would willingly, gladly have gone into that operating room in my place. And I was thankful I was in that bed instead of standing there having to watch one of them being wheeled away to surgery.

Very soon a nurse came in with the pre-surgery injection.

Almost immediately I felt the warmth and comfort of the Demerol begin to spread through my body.

"Let's have prayer," I heard Papa say through the haze that was beginning to envelop me. As he prayed aloud, I felt the love and prayers of the others who were gathered around my bed. I was soothed and lifted up into a state of perfect peace.

Too soon it was time to go. Jim kissed me; I smiled as brightly as possible for Ross and Laura. And I prayed for each of those people who were so dear to me, for I knew their hurt would be greater than mine in the next few hours, especially if the news was bad.

And I thought: *If I live, no matter what the outcome, I'll come down from surgery into this warm circle of love. If I should die before I wake, I'll enter into the beauty of my Savior's love. What more could anyone ask?*

I've never been inside an operating room of any other hospital, yet I'm sure the surgical floor of Memorial can't be beat! There are seven operating rooms—completely modern, shiny, clean, and well-equipped—a large recovery room, a doctors' lounge, etc. Several years ago I had attended the open house celebrating the completion of this new facility, little dreaming that one of the daily human dramas enacted here would be mine.

This morning I looked eagerly around to catch glimpses of an otherwise off-limits domain. How I wanted to get up and walk around, maybe even watch the surgery underway in the room next to mine! Probably, I thought, all this would become routine, maybe even boring, if I were up here all the time likes these O.R. nurses. Certainly it appeared so to them. But today, just *today*, how exciting it would be to be a spectator!

I could have been a mannequin for all the attention anyone paid as I was scooted from the stretcher to the operating table. No one seemed to notice. Do they think I'm asleep? "Hi," I said to no one in particular. Startled, several heads turned.

"Hello," someone said, but they all seemed embarrassed. *Maybe they're not supposed to talk*, I decided, so I shut up and just looked.

A woman with eyes (that's all I could see; everything else was swathed in green) came in and introduced herself as the anesthetist. She began to hook me up to all kinds of tubes. "Don't put me to sleep yet. I have to see Dr. Garrett," I cautioned, and she nodded.

I was so cold I could hardly keep my teeth from chattering. "How can you work in here with it so cold?" I asked. No reply. (*Am I asleep or are they?*)

"Ready to go to sleep?" Lifting my head I saw Dr. Garrett standing in the doorway. He was dressed all in green from his tennis shoes to his little green cap. His hands were gloved and held away from his body in front of his chest.

"You look like a leprechaun," I said, amused. "Yes, I'm ready."

"Okay, see you later."

The anesthetist began the medication. "You'll be asleep in just a few seconds."

Quickly I looked around. "Dr. Garrett?"

"What now?" he feigned exasperation, grinning.

"Don't forget to wake me up."

*   *   *

Faintly, from far away I heard my name being called. "Susan? Susan. Take a few more deep breaths for me now." *More deep*

breaths? *Have I taken some already? She said I'd remember.* . . .
I drifted off to sleep again.

"Susan!" More insistent now. "Take some deep breaths for
me. It's time to wake up." *No. I just went to sleep. Dr. Garrett is
going to operate. Oh, no! Don't let him operate yet! I'm not asleep!*

"Susan? Listen to me. It's over. You're in the recovery room."
Slowly I opened my eyes. This was *not* the operating room. There
was a man in the bed next to mine, snoring loudly.

I began to *feel*. "I'm so cold. Please get me a blanket. I'm so
cold." My teeth were chattering so I could hardly speak.

"You've already got three blankets. You'll be warmer soon."

I've got to think. I've got to wake up. Closing my eyes, pretending to sleep, I tried to get my head together. *I'm not in heaven. I
wouldn't have to listen to that snoring in heaven. I must still be alive!*

Okay. I'm alive and I'm cold. The nurse isn't looking. Slowly I
moved my right hand under the covers toward my left breast.
Bandages, lots of them. *I can't really tell. Oh! Pain!*

Quickly I moved my hand. *All right. I'm alive, I'm cold, I hurt.*
"*Big whoop,*" *as Ross would say. Now what?*

"Susan? Take some deep breaths."

As I struggled to comply, it came to me. *I know, I know! I'll
ask the nurse!*

"Nurse? What happened?" *Simple! Why didn't I think of that
before?*

"Dr. Garrett will be here in just a minute. He'll tell you all
about it."

*So much for that brilliant maneuver. Activate Plan B. Okay,
sweet nurse. Here comes the biggy.*

"What time is it?"

"Oh, about 1:30."

Suddenly I didn't feel so smart. *Six hours. Six hours since I came up to surgery. Even an idiot could figure out what that means.*

I heard Dr. Garrett say my name; I didn't want to open my eyes. (*If I don't open my eyes, he'll go away.*)

"Susan?" He said my name so gently. I could hear the pain in his voice. (*He's hurting, too. He doesn't want to tell me this. I have to help him. It's not his fault.*)

"I *know*. It's okay. I know." I looked up and he was smiling—a strained smile, but a smile—and I smiled back.

"You really messed up my day," he said, *trying*. I wanted to reply in kind: *Business slow this morning, huh? Thought you'd get in a little extra practice?* But all that came out was, "I'm sorry."

"I'm sorry, too. I'm so sorry."

There was an awkward silence. I had my eyes closed, fighting tears. I don't know what he was doing.

"Listen," he said, struggling for words. "I have to tell you about it; then you can go back to sleep. It was malignant. I did just what I said I'd do if it turned out that way. There didn't seem to be any in the lymph nodes; I'm sure we got it all, but we'll have a more definite report in a few days."

"Does Jim know?"

"I told your family before I did the operation. They know."

What else was there to say?

"Dr. Garrett?"

"Hmmm?"

"I'm so *cold*. Why is it so cold in here?" And I went back to sleep.

Chapter Seven

It is vital, after a Halsted radical mastectomy, to begin exercising immediately, to strengthen the auxiliary muscles of the arm that take over for the removed pectorals. . . . Most (women) who had had the Halsted radical said it was difficult for them to reeducate auxiliary muscles to take over for the pectorals, which had been removed. For them regaining the full use of the arm had top priority; pain and cosmetics were secondary.

Breast Cancer: A Personal History
and an Investigative Report
Rose Kushner

He doth give his joy to all:
He becomes an Infant small,
He becomes a Man of Woe,
He doth feel the sorrow too.

Think not thou canst sigh a sigh,
And thy Maker is not by:
Think not thou canst weep a tear,
And thy Maker is not near.

Oh, he gives to us his joy,
That our grief he may destroy.
Till our grief is fled and gone
He doth sit by us and moan.

William Blake

Be merciful unto me, O God,
be merciful unto me: for my soul trusteth in thee:
yea, in the shadow of thy wings will I make my refuge,
until these calamities be overpast.

Psalm 57:1

When I opened my eyes again, I was back in my room. Everything was hazy; all I knew with absolute certainty was that I was cold. Nurses hovered around me, adjusting and checking the flow of the blood that was dripping through tubes into my hand, propping my left side up, bringing me blankets, murmuring words of comfort.

Then Jim was there, looking tired and drawn, his face blurred through my tears as he bent over to kiss me. Ross and Laura stretched to reach me over the raised bars of the bed; and although the worried looks on their faces tore at my heart, I managed to smile to reassure them. My mother and father came in next and kissed me; Jim's parents also appeared, ghostlike, through the mist of my semi-awareness. Like a parade, rank upon rank, two by two, others followed to assure me of their concern and love: Jeannie and Mike, Ken and Linda, Brother Larry (our pastor in Diboll), my brother Steve, and many others.

They had to come in in shifts, a few at a time, but Jim entered first and never left. (My memory is dim, but if I know my Mama, once she got in *she* didn't leave either!) Jim held my right hand, trying to warm it, and Mama massaged my feet. I drifted in and out of consciousness, becoming more and more aware of the ever-increasing pain.

It seemed an eternity before I got warm. Another eternity passed before I got an injection for the pain. The rest of the afternoon passed in seesaw fashion: I awoke to pain and the comforting awareness of Jim and Mama; I got a pain shot and waited eagerly for the blessedness of sleep and absence of pain and thought.

Soon it was night. I realized that a cot had been brought into the room. "What's going on?" I asked.

"Your mother is going to spend the night with you," Jim said softly. "I tried to get her to go home, but she wouldn't hear of it. I even *promised* I'd take good care of you!" he joked. "I'll just go out to Ken and Linda's and be back early in the morning."

Even in my befuddled state of mind, I realized what was happening; I was so grateful for the depth of Jim's love, not only for me but for my mother. He knew she *had* to stay—I was her "little girl." And although he had every right to insist on staying himself, he graciously acknowledged *her* right as a mother to care for her child. And as much as I loved him and wanted him near me, there was no one in the world I needed that night as much as I needed my mother.

"Thank you, honey," I whispered, and he left me with a kiss.

All through that long afternoon and evening I had been vomiting. Alternately Jim or Mama had held the little crescent-shaped pan to my face, cooled my forehead with a cloth dipped in ice water, or fed me tiny pieces of ice trying to quench my terrible thirst. Now it was my mother who had the wearying, constant vigil. She lay down occasionally but when I called her name, she was by my side immediately.

I thought of the little saying, "God could not be everywhere, so He created mothers." Those words took on a new depth of meaning that long May night. I did not see God, but He was there; soothing me through my mother's voice, holding my hand with my mother's hand, keeping a constant watch through her eyes. And when she shed tears that she thought I didn't notice, they were His tears, too.

*   *   *

All through that first day and night I had not even thought of the magnitude of what had happened to me. The urgency of my body's needs, discomforts, and demands pushed all else from a place of immediate concern. Getting the pain stopped was much more vital than the fact that I had cancer. Finding a comfortable position was, without a doubt, of greater magnitude than how I would adjust to one breast instead of two. Being warm was considerably more important than whether or not I would still be sexy and desirable. All of these problems, and a multitude more, would arise later, but tonight they didn't matter one bit.

One of the urgent demands my body made that night caused extreme distress but provided the only hint of humor I recall. I needed desperately to go to the bathroom, but of course I couldn't get up. The obvious solution was the bedpan. Nothing doing! I tried for what seemed hours. Nurses poured warm water over me; Mama turned on the faucet in the bathroom. Nothing helped.

Finally, when the misery was more than I could bear another minute, a nurse came to catheterize me. I apologized for being so much trouble.

"It's all Mama's fault," I told her. "When she taught me not to wet the bed, she taught me *good*."

*   *   *

The seemingly endless night passed into day, and that day into many more days much the same. A profusion of memories remain with me of those ten days I was hospitalized after surgery. Many of them are mere fragments, gray-shaded and vague, etched on my mind so delicately that just a year's aging has almost succeeded in erasing the pictures they made. Some memories are watercolored, gentle and soothing to recall, never to be forgotten because of their soft beauty. And indelibly splashed on my mind's canvas are the brilliant acrylic-type recollections that compose the major part of my hospital-stay memorabilia. Harsh sometimes, vivid always, these reminiscences represent the things that are too beautiful, too important, or too unpleasant to forget.

I will never forget the wonderful staff of women, nurses and aides alike, who cared for me during those two weeks. Some of the names are forgotten, but their acts of kindness and concern are not. As busy as they were, they always were cheerful and helpful; they treated me as a person rather than just a patient; they gave me wonderful bedbaths and rubbed lotion into my tired and aching legs and back. They showered me with compliments, boosted my morale by helping me look my best, and even washed my hair for me in bed. They "oohed" and "aahed" over the huge array of flowers and plants, arranging and watering them for me; they provided tape for the hundreds of cards I received, even helping to put them on the walls around my bed. They gave me their hearts and their love, and I'm eternally grateful for those hard-working, selfless women who nursed me through that emotionally and physically shattering period of my life.

I had no idea then that these women would be caring for me in much the same way three more times within the coming year. Or that my mother and I would reverse roles, and in a few months *I* would be the one on the cot and *she* the patient in the hospital bed. How thankful I am that God does not show us the future, even when we long to know what lies ahead. In my case, even a glimpse of the coming months would have been more than I could bear. But by giving us grace "unto the day" and *faith* for the future rather than *knowledge* of it, God enables us to endure and even, amazingly, to rejoice when the unexpected becomes reality.

*   *   *

Thursday morning, following surgery on Wednesday, my normally independent and strong-willed personality began to assert itself. "I am going to get up and go to the bathroom," I stated matter-of-factly to Mama.

"Wait. I'll call a nurse and we'll *ask* first," she replied calmly, but with authority.

I hadn't planned on doing that, nor did I think it was necessary. But not only had Mama taught me not to wet the bed, she had taught me to *mind*. "Yes, ma'am," I said meekly. And I waited.

A nurse came promptly, and after being assured that it was a proven matter of record already that the bedpan and I did not function well together, she left to get permission from the doctor for me to get up. Returning shortly, she said grudgingly, "Okay. We'll *try*. But let's go slow and don't you ever try to get up without one of us in here."

That was the joke of the year, I soon discovered. As if I *could* go by myself! Aside from my being unbelievably weak and lightheaded, it would have been physically impossible for me to unhook the intravenous bag from its lofty perch. I also discovered I had a foreign object attached to my body by two tubes stuck into the bandages and going who-knows-where. The nurses' term for this little contraption was a *pancake*. (Actually it was a Hemo-Vac, a round, pouch-like gadget that exerted a vacuum to draw out serous fluid, which otherwise would accumulate and cause pain and swelling.)

After satisfying my initial curiosity about the pancake by following the clear plastic tubes all the way up under my gown to where they disappeared into *me*, I sat up for a few minutes before attempting to stand. Then, confidently, with a nurse on one arm and Mama on the other, I stood up. And *immediately* sat back down. This was going to be worse than I thought. Maybe I just ought to wet the bed.

I made it on the next attempt. What a sight we must have been! The nurse held the "sugar water" high above my head; Mama carried the pancake, and I held on to each of them for dear life. When I finally got back in my bed, I thought, *That was the most difficult thing I've ever tried to do. Just to get to the bathroom and back!* And there was nothing—no small voice, no premonition, *nothing* to warn me: *You ain't seen nothin' yet!*

As for now, content to be alive, well-cared-for, showered with gifts, flowers, cards, *attention*, I was in a state of near euphoria. *I did it!* I congratulated myself proudly. *I have survived "The Surgery Most Dreaded by Women" and come through with flying colors.* It wasn't half bad—not nearly so bad as we'd all been led to believe. Why, I was going to be just fine. Adjustment? To what? After all, to an intelligent woman, who has her priorities straight, what can it *possibly* matter if she has one less breast?

I continued to pat myself on the back for my good behavior. I wore a permanent smile. Then, several days after surgery, it happened. Dr. Garrett removed the heavy, post-surgical dressing in favor of a smaller one. For the first time I saw my incision. It was then I realized that not only was I going to be playing by a few new rules, but *I was in a whole new ball game.*

"You really did it up right, didn't you? Talk about mutilated!" I wisecracked.

I almost wished I hadn't been so eager to see it; yet I couldn't take my eyes off the ugly, red wound that began at my shoulder (just far enough out to be visible in a sleeveless blouse) and curved to run diagonally, brutally, almost to my waist. The black stitches were in stark contrast to the brilliant red and white of my tender, outraged skin. Bones I never knew I had were visible, and I could see my heart thumping strongly under the thin layer of skin.

This, then, is what it's all about. *This* is a mastectomy. I never would have dreamed it would look like this. I continued to stare at my body as if it belonged to someone else. I was hardly conscious of the fact that Dr. Garrett was removing a few of the stitches. I saw the two drainage tubes, at least a quarter of an inch wide, stuck into my side like needles in a pin chushion. *Why don't they hurt? That looks awful—why doesn't it hurt?*

I couldn't lift my left arm to do a thorough check, but from what I could see by craning my neck, it appeared that my entire armpit was gone. The large muscle connecting my arm to my chest had disappeared. My whole left side was concave, and I wondered how in the world I would be able to camouflage the terrible deformity.

I realized that Dr. Garrett was speaking, and I tried to concentrate on what he was saying. "It's not pretty, I know, but when the wound heals and the scar fades it won't be so bad. Right now you just need to think about getting your strength back. New muscles have to be trained to take over for the missing ones. Start lifting your arm a little more each day. If it's okay with you, I'll give permission for a Reach to Recovery volunteer to come by and tell you about some good exercises and other things you'll want to know."

All I got out of that whole spiel was the one word *exercise*. *He's got to be kidding*, I thought. For three days now I'd tried desperately to keep my arm folded, winglike, against my body. That was the way it hurt the least. To think of moving it *on purpose* was ridiculous.

"Dr. Garrett," I stated as calmly as possible, "it *hurts* to move it."

"I know that." (*How to you know? How do you know?*) "But if you don't begin moving that arm you will be permanently crippled. That arm will never be normal again, and it will be nobody's fault but your own. If you'll do what I say, no matter how hard it is, I guarantee you'll be able to do anything you could do before."

Again, only part of what he said penetrated my mind—the phrase "permanently crippled"—but that was enough. Not *me*. That is definitely not for me if I can help it, and he says I can. Almost before he left the room, I was trying to straighten my arm. Trying to clench my fist. Trying to wipe the tears of pain and frustration from my eyes.

*   *   *

I was still very weak. Dr. Garrett had told me that I'd had three pints of blood during surgery (and another in my room) because "everywhere I touched you, you bled." But after the second day, Mama and I were able to make it to the bathroom without calling a nurse, and when the I.V. was removed, and a few more days had passed, I could go alone. *Big deal*, I thought. I'd never have dreamed going to the bathroom by myself would be a major accomplishment and cause me so much pride. I wondered if I felt the same pride when I was a toddler and first used the potty instead of my pants.

Jim stayed the third night with me, allowing Mama, who was satisfied that I was going to make it, to go home and get some rest. Jim and I had a good time, despite the circumstances. It was like spending the night in a fancy hotel, minus the kids, except we were sleeping in separate beds! We didn't discuss anything very serious; however, I did show him what was visible of my incision. I had to get that over with right off the bat. I watched him carefully. I saw no disgust; he didn't turn away; he didn't say, "I'm filing for divorce tomorrow."

"I always liked the other one better anyway," he said. "Now move that arm. We're going water skiing next week."

We were especially happy that night, for Dr. Garrett had come in earlier with good news about the final lab test.

"There was no lymph node involvement. The cancer was an early lesion and had not spread beyond the breast. That's the best news we could possibly have gotten."

I didn't realize just how good that news was until months later as I began to read all I could find about breast cancer. No lymph node involvement meant I had an 80% chance of a five-year cancer-free survival as compared to a 40-45% chance if the malignancy had spread to the lymph nodes in the axilla.

Saturday Jim's older sister, Pat, came from Bryan where she and her husband, Tom, live. Pat's arrival began a very special period of my convalescence. Pat and I had always loved each other, but due to circumstances and distances separating us, we'd never been together for long at any one time. The three days and nights she spent with me were love-and-laughter filled—a time of caring and sharing with one another. No one could have been dearer to me, or more thoughtful, than my sister-in-law was those few days.

Friends continued to come by constantly. There are no restrictions to visiting hours at Memorial, nor to how many visitors can crowd into a room at one time. Many times my room was filled to capacity, but it kept me so busy trying to play the hostess and be interested and cheerful that I did not resent it. In fact, I welcomed it; the steady flow of well-wishers gave me no time to think. Having someone near all the time gave me no time to feel sorry for myself. I still had not had a good cry. I knew I needed it, but so far there hadn't been an opportunity!

My main concern, during my entire hospital stay, was the children. I knew they were being well-cared-for and well-loved. Jim's other sister, Jan, was seeing to that, as far as the little ones were concerned. Ross and Laura were staying home and were old enough to understand I would be home soon.

But the babies—and I still considered one-year-old Lana and three-year-old Rick *babies*—couldn't really understand where Mommy was. Or if she would come back. *Especially* Rick, poor little vagabond, who was just beginning to realize what "mommy" and "home" meant. I could hardly stand to think of what *he* might be feeling. This caused me more pain than my surgery. I tried to force my feelings of love across the miles to him: *Oh, Rick, my precious little son. Mommy loves you. I'm coming home soon. I didn't leave you. I didn't give you away.*

And to God I pleaded, *Please don't let him be hurt any more. Calm his fears. Let him be happy. Take good care of him for me. Please.*

*   *   *

Several days after my surgery I picked up my Bible, determined to make time for a few quiet moments with God. This seemed like a good opportunity. It was just after my noontime visitors had gone; normally I could expect a little quiet "nap time" for at least an hour. Pat had gone to the cafeteria for her lunch after having helped me with mine.

There are so many times in my life when I find myself skipping along life's way, doing quite well really, and then the thoughts occur: How long has it been since I sat down and read my Bible? How long has it been since I really sat down and prayed—not the little here-and-there snatches of conversation I offer up frequently, often without conscious thought, but a real worship and praise *sacrifice* of prayer? I have to remind myself that although things have been running smoothly, I've needed God just the same. And then I realize He's been there all along, making that way smooth, and I haven't had the courtesy to sit down and thank Him for it.

"Cruising for a bruising" is the expression I use in my own mind when I realize this has happened. I'm fixing to stub my toe for sure! Some great temptation is going to plop itself down in plain view, or a minor irritation is going to blow itself up to preposterous proportions, and I'm not going to be ready because I haven't been "putting on my armor" by studying the Bible and asking God's daily protection from evil.

So I stop, get my Bible, and get down to business with God. (*Thank You, God, for parents, teachers, books, friends, anyone who's ever helped me realize how important it is to study Your Word and have fellowship with You. How does anyone survive without it?*)

This afternoon I was absolutely starved for a good talk with God. How grateful I was for a few minutes by myself. And with that eager frame of mind, seeking and expecting God's comfort, I received one of the greatest blessings He's ever given me. For as I opened my Bible, the pages fell open to Philippians 3. My eyes were riveted immediately on one section, verses 20 and 21, which say:

> For our conversation is in heaven; from whence also we look for the Savior, the Lord Jesus Christ:

> Who shall change our *vile body*, that it may be fashioned like unto his glorious body, according to the working whereby he is able even to subdue all things unto himself.

Talk about vile bodies! I had one! This verse was written for me. What a blessing! What a promise! Someday my "vile body" would be changed and made glorious. I would not always look like this. This temporary body, and it *is* that, is just a shell that houses my spirit. When life *really* begins, when we've ended our brief stay here, we will be totally free of these bodies we have now. Oh, joy! How exciting that is to me!

If there are any two aspects of Christianity that really get me excited, they are the second coming and life after death—the former I feel sure will be soon; the latter will be great *whenever* it comes. Death holds absolutely no fear for me; this is not because I'm a "super saint," which I most definitely am not, but because the absence of fear is a special gift from God to me. He has given me complete, unswerving assurance in my innermost being that there is life after death and that it will be great for those who are His children. That belief, and the same concrete assurance and anticipation of His coming again soon, are my special strong points—my *bonus* points of Christianity. There are other principles of theology I'm not so positive about, and I don't want to argue any of them. But I know what I know, and I thank God for the knowledge.

Here in this hospital, in these two verses, God gave me my gifts again: the anticipation of Jesus' coming again and the assurance of *newness* in all things (even vile bodies!) in heaven when life here is over.

And as if that weren't enough, He had led me this afternoon to Philippians, my favorite book in the Bible. I thumbed eagerly through the much-used pages, noticing favorite underlined verses:

Chapter 1

Verse 6: Being confident of this very thing, that he which hath begun a good work in you will perform it until the day of Jesus Christ. *(Be patient with me, everybody. I'm still under construction!)*

Verse 20: . . .so now also Christ shall be magnified in my body, whether it be by life, or by death. *(This body? Can He be magnified in this body? Hmmm . . . maybe better now than before.)*

Verse 21: For to me to live is Christ, and to die is gain. *(To die is gain, I know. I know, too, that I am alive by Christ's mercy. But does this mean, perhaps, that I should live as if it were Christ who lived, rather than me?)*

Chapter 2

Verse 14: Do all things without murmurings and disputings. *(Easy here in the hospital—much harder in ordinary, everyday life.)*

Verse 15: . . .that ye may be blameless and harmless, the sons of God, without rebuke, in the midst of a crooked and perverse nation, among whom ye shine as lights in the world. *(Just let me be a witness for You as often as I can, Lord. I've failed You so often; I will again. But help me be more consistent.)*

Chapter 4

Verse 4: Rejoice in the Lord always: and again I say rejoice!
(Always? Even with cancer? Even in pain? Always!)
Verse 7: And the peace of God, which passeth all understanding,
shall keep your hearts and minds through Christ Jesus. *(It is
beyond all human comprehension, Father, at least my comprehension, how you have kept me in perfect peace through all this.)*
Verse 11: I have learned, in whatsoever state I am, therewith to
be content. *(You're ahead of me there, Paul. But I'm on my way!)*
Verse 13: I can do all things through Christ which strengtheneth
me. *(Even raise my arm above my head again! Someday soon!)*

I thought of Mrs. Arthur DeLoach, a beautiful Christian lady
whose husband had been pastor of First Baptist Church in Lufkin
for many years. Many years ago I had studied Philippians under
her leadership in a Bible study group that met in her home. Notes
and comments in my Bible were testimony to her wisdom and
understanding of the text. She taught me the beauty of "joy in the
Lord"—not just through her teachings, but through the radiant joy
that shone from her beautiful face when she spoke of the Lord.

A mental telegram flew through the spaces separating us: *Mrs.
DeLoach, thank you so much for sharing your home, your love,
your knowledge with me. Thanks for your part in preparing me for
this special time in my life.*

*And thank You, wise and loving heavenly Father, for Your
Book, which has once again met the need of my heart.*

Chapter Eight

We have spoken before of the lymph nodes of the internal mammary chain, which lie behind the breastbone and into which may drain cancer cells from tumors in the inner half of the breast. These nodes lie behind the ribs. They cannot be felt through the chest wall, and they cannot be detected by X rays. Therefore, if there is cancer in these nodes, it may not become apparent until it grows through the chest wall and forms a tumor there.

Since recurrence of cancer in the chest wall is hard to control by either radiation or surgery, some surgeons have advised routine radiation of this area after the original operation in all patients who have tumors in the inner quadrant of the breast.

What Women Should Know About the Breast Cancer Controversy
George Crile, Jr., M.D.

Tears are the safety valve of the heart when too much pressure is laid on it.

Albert Smith

And not only so, but we glory in tribulations also: knowing that tribulation worketh patience; and patience, experience; and experience, hope: and hope maketh not ashamed; because the love of God is shed abroad in our hearts by the Holy Ghost which is given unto us.

Romans 5:3-5

Two separate incidents intruded into the idyllic, dreamlike world of the hospital routine that caused me to realize, for the first time, the extent of what had happened to me. The first was a visit by the Reach to Recovery volunteer; the second, a visit from Dr. Kistler from the radiation center. Until then, perhaps because of sedation, maybe because I just hadn't been ready to face reality, I had drifted from day to day, enjoying the care I'd received, the visitors, mail, calls, etc., that came steadily. After all, the surgery was over and, aside from a great deal of discomfort, I was doing fine.

When the nurse stuck her head in the door and asked what size bra I wore, I thought she had gone crazy. After getting my answer she ducked out, smiling mysteriously, as quickly as she had appeared. *What next?* I thought. *They've asked me everything imaginable. Guess they'll want my shoe size next.*

Later the same day another nurse entered my room carrying one of the stands used to hold intravenous bags. Seeing my horrified expression, she quickly assured me that it wasn't for *that*! "The Reach to Recovery volunteer wants it here when she comes this afternoon," she offered as explanation.

My curiosity was definitely aroused; I could hardly wait till she arrived. I'd heard of the program, sponsored by the American

Cancer Society, and I knew the volunteers were women who had successfully adjusted to mastectomies and wanted to help others who were facing the same problems. The program sounded good. And, as usual, any apprehension I felt was overshadowed by my ever-present curiosity. Another new experience! Next time I read about Reach to Recovery I'd know all about it!

I was alone today. Pat had gone home; the weekend was over and she had to get back to her classroom. I was dozing after a good noon meal when I heard a knock on the door.

"Come in," I said, instantly alert, expecting my volunteer.

A lovely, well-groomed woman about my mother's age entered, smiling.

"Kathleen! How nice to see you again!" I exclaimed, and I meant it. This woman, Kathleen Cromwell, had been in that long-ago Bible class at Mrs. DeLoach's. I hadn't seen her since then; in fact, I had never seen her outside those classes. I was not really too surprised that she knew I was there; several members of the group had been by to see me.

"Susan?" she said. "Is that really you?" (*Now what did she mean by that?*) She continued, a little flustered: "When they called and gave me your name, I knew it sounded familiar. I thought, *That can't be the same Susan Nethery!*"

Puzzled, I said, "Kathleen, I'm glad to see you, but I don't have the faintest idea what you are talking about."

"I'm your Reach to Recovery volunteer! Isn't that something? You are my very first case, and I was so nervous about it. Isn't it a coincidence that it's *you?*"

I was stunned. That was more than a coincidence—that was God's hand working again. How wonderful it was to have someone I knew, a Christian and a friend, to help me learn to adjust to the difficulties I had to face in the days ahead. Both of us were immediately at ease in a situation that had caused us both anxiety previously.

I hadn't known about her surgery, almost two years ago, and she had not known until she got here that I was who she thought I was. We spent several enthusiastic, enjoyable minutes "catching up" before she began her presentation.

Katheen affirmed what Dr. Garrett had expressed: "It's hard to believe now when you're in pain, plastered with bandages and held together by stitches, but you will be able to resume normal activities in time."

She told me, briefly, of her personal experience. It was apparent that she had, indeed, regained full use of her arm. It was also apparent that it was *not* apparent that she had had a mastectomy. No one would ever have guessed by looking.

However, I wanted to say but didn't: "You are much older than I am. You probably don't wear two-piece bathing suits, clingy knit dresses, halter tops, and T-shirts. I do." (Correction: I did.) "You don't have small children at home. I do. Do you have any idea of the problems that entails? I doubt that you enjoy playing volleyball, basketball, or water skiing. What can you tell me about how my surgery will affect that area of my life? And how about sexual relations with my husband? I don't feel that I can discuss this with you. Not because I doubt your ability to understand and advise, but because I would be a little embarrassed because of our age difference. Dear Kathleen," I said to her in my mind, "I'm so glad you are here and I appreciate it. But how I wish you were my age!"

To my amazement, though, the information this dear lady *did* have was so helpful and reassuring that I forgot my disappointment about the things I felt she could not help me with. The little white bag she brought contained an assortment of goodies: an excellent book by Terese Lasser, founder of the Reach to Recovery program; a leisure bra (in my size—end of that mystery!) with a soft little dacron-fluff-filled pocket for the proper side; a red rubber ball with an attached elastic string; a rope pulley with tongue-depressor handles.

Positioning the I.V. stand in front of her, Kathleen showed me an exercise to do with the rope she had brought. This same exercise could be adapted to a closet door or shower curtain rod at home. She demonstrated several other exercises, including one with the red ball, stressing again and again their importance to complete recovery. She told me of the Reach to Recovery "yardstick" that would indicate the end of the need for formal exercises: arms raised straight up over the head, hands touching flat and being able to fasten your bra or tie an apron behind you!

After assuring me that she would see me again before I went home and insisting that I call her, day or night, if I needed anything, she gave me a gentle hug and left. Eagerly I picked up the book. I had glanced through it briefly when she handed it to me and had been fascinated by many interesting and promising section topics: Why Me?, Sexuality and Femininity, The Man in Your Life, Your Family, Everything You Need to Know About Breast Forms, and Hand and Arm Care. I read the booklet from cover to cover without pause. It was very helpful and encouraging, but several weeks passed before I realized that it only skimmed the surface of the pool of problems that would be popping up.

*   *   *

During evening rounds that day, Dr. Garrett casually mentioned that I could expect another special visitor the next day.

Noting the serious expression on his face just in time to stifle my upcoming wisecrack, I put on *my* serious face and said, "Oh?"

"Yeah," he replied, a little uncomfortably, I thought. "Dr. Bill Kistler, a radiologist from downstairs, will be coming by to talk to you about some cobalt treatments. We think you should have some strictly as a precaution. There was no lymph node involvement, as I told you, but there is a chain of nodes behind your breastbone that we couldn't check without really massive surgery that wasn't called for in your case."

Managing to close my mouth, I swallowed hard and concentrated on dredging up from my memory file all the bits and pieces of accumulated trivia relating to radiation, cobalt, and cancer treatment. I found precious little. What I did find didn't make me very happy: hair loss, burned skin, treatment for inoperable cancer.

"You're not lying to me about anything are you?" I asked suspiciously.

"I don't ever lie to a patient. I certainly wouldn't try it with *you!*" he protested. "Just wait till you talk to Dr. Kistler. He'll explain it all to you." He threw in one last remark as he went out the door: "You'll like him!"

Carefully pondering all he'd said, I came to a conclusion: "There's no way for me to know what's true and what's not, no way to know what's right and what's wrong; I'll just have to trust the Lord and Dr. Garrett. Neither of them has let me down yet."

Dr. Connell made her evening check and reaffirmed what Dr. Garrett had said. Not just about the need for the cobalt, but about my liking Dr. Kistler! Intrigued now, my curiosity aroused again, I looked forward eagerly to meeting this sure-to-be-liked Dr. Kistler.

*　　*　　*

I bathed and "dressed" with special care next morning. I was trying hard to look nice each day anyway, but meeting a new doctor called for a little extra attention. I was able to take a real bath now, simply taking care not to get my bandages wet.

I recalled that first tub bath after surgery. My sister-in-law, Linda, was visiting at the time, and I enlisted her aid in shaving my underarms! There was just no way I could do it. I couldn't do the right side because my left arm didn't work right, and I couldn't do the left side because my right hand couldn't hold my left arm up and shave under it at the same time! If it hadn't been such a ridiculous situation, I probably would have cried from the agony of it. Not only did it hurt to have my arm lifted high enough to shave it, but the total "deadness" of the area gave me the eeriest feeling I've ever experienced. I was glad when it was over. I'm sure Linda was, too, bless her!

I was able to do a one-handed job on my hair and even do a fair job with makeup. I put on a fresh gown (Linda kept them laundered for me) and the fluffy quilted bedjacket Sandra Pouland, a friend from Diboll, had given me. I was so grateful for that gift. It was the only thing I had to wear that I didn't look conspicuously lopsided in. That right breast, so small *before* surgery, now seemed Raquel-Welch-sized, embarrassing me by just being there in such proud contrast to the flat nothingness of the other side.

Critically I looked at myself in the small bathroom mirror. Covered this way I looked "normal." A smile flickered across my face as I recalled a remark Jim had made to me over the weekend. Coming into the room, he saw me "prettied up" for the first time since surgery. "Hey, he whistled appreciatively. "You're not *half bad*!"

It took me a few seconds to catch his double meaning; when I did, I threw a pillow at him.

*   *   *

Dr. Kistler hadn't been in my room five minutes before I decided: "I like this man!" It wasn't because he was tall, although I noticed that immediately. (It's amazing the habits you carry over from childhood. I reached my height of 5′9″ at an early age; I was taller than the girls and almost all the boys from junior high school through high school. To this day, shame on me, the first thing I notice about a man is whether or not I could wear heels on a date with him! Dr. Kistler qualified.)

It wasn't just because he was handsome, but I noticed that, too. (They may have amputated my breast, but my eyes were intact!) But then I've known a lot of good-looking men who were very uninteresting and unlikable.

No, I decided, it has to be his manner. He's a gentleman and obviously a gentle man. His eyes are warm and caring. He has a soft laugh, which he uses a lot, and he's just plain old down-home *nice*. Before our visit was over, I knew a good bit about him: he was a Christian (a Methodist, but I decided to let him treat me anyway!); he had more kids than I did, one of them in college (he must use Grecian Formula on that dark hair of his!); and he used to be a "real" doctor before going into radiology!

We didn't get into an in-depth discussion of my treatments. I suppose there really wasn't that much I needed to know at the time. It had been decided that I needed cobalt by people who knew far more than I about it. So, as far as I was concerned, that settled it.

I questioned him about side effects.

"With the small amount of radiation you'll be getting, I don't anticipate any."

"How many treatments?"

"You'll get twenty-five, one a day for five weeks."

"When do they start?"

"About a week after you go home."

That was about it. And that was enough. For then.

*　　*　　*

Cancer . . . cancer . . . cancer. . . . The awful word swirled round and round in my head as I lay trying to rest after dinner. All my life I had feared it. Oh, I hadn't gone around worrying about it; in fact, I rarely ever thought of it. I had just always felt that someday I'd have cancer, and die from it, the same way Jim has always thought he'd die from a heart attack. My daddy's mother died from cancer; that's probably where my fears originated. But now that the fear had become a reality, I couldn't believe it. Isn't that strange? I believed it more before it happened!

I turned and twisted, trying unsuccessfully to find a comfortable position. My mind in a turmoil, I tried to push my panicky feelings aside and recapture the tranquility and peace that I'd felt up until then. But questions tumbled all over each other, clamoring for answers that weren't there. *Why is this happening to me? Did I do something to cause this? What if I die? What will happen to the children? Why would God give me those two new babies if I wasn't going to be here to rear them? Why now? How will we ever be able to pay for all this? Why didn't we take out a cancer policy with our other insurance? Will I be able to adjust? Will Jim? Where is God?*

I rang the buzzer to call a nurse.

"May I help you?" the voice came quietly through the intercom.

"I want to see the head nurse, please," I said, my voice quivering.

She appeared promptly, concerned. This nurse, young and pretty, had been especially helpful and supportive. I knew she would understand the request I was about to make.

"I am so tired," I explained wearily, on the verge of tears, "and I haven't had a good cry since I've been here. I really need it. Will you get me something for pain—my side is hurting and I haven't had anything today—and then would you put a 'No Visitors' sign on the door? I just need a little time to be by myself."

I could see a worried look in her eyes. I continued, "Don't be worried about me. I'm not depressed, I'm not worried, I'm not angry. I'm just so tired and I need to be alone. I wanted to warn you so that when I started crying you wouldn't all come running in here!"

"I understand," she said gently, and I could see that she did. "I'll be right back. Can you hold the waterworks a few more minutes?"

While she was gone I got up and pulled the shades to shut out the sunlight and got back into bed clutching a handful of kleenex. "All I need now is some violin music," I thought ruefully. "Otherwise the stage is set for my great scene."

The nurse was back very soon, bringing my medication and carrying a sign under her arm. I swallowed the pills.

"If you need me, just buzz," she said before leaving. "Enjoy your cry and get a good nap."

For several minutes I lay there debating whether or not I should have put up that "No Visitors" sign. *What if someone from out of town comes to see me? What if someone I'd really like to visit with shows up? What if someone brings me a present and takes it back home!*

Dr. Garrett had told me previously, in commenting on the large number of visitors I was having, that he wasn't going to tell the nurses to put the sign up. But he told me it was available and to stick it on the door if I felt the need. Okay, today I felt the need.

I began to feel very alone. I liked it. Anticipating even an hour of quiet, darkness, and being by myself was such a pleasure that I almost couldn't get a good cry worked up! Eventually, though, as I relaxed, the emotions I'd kept locked inside for almost two weeks came surging forward, demanding release. Eagerly I welcomed the "flood" I knew was forthcoming. I knew, as every woman knows, there's nothing like tears to wash the blues away, to change a mood, or to clean the windows of the soul and let the light shine in again.

The tears trickled down my cheeks as I began to pray: *Thank you, dear Father, for tears. Thank You for giving us this way to release emotions, show joy and pain, ease frustration and heartache.*

Tears flowed from my eyes now, and still I prayed: *Please understand, God, that these tears are not directed against you. I'm not mad at You and I'm not angry about what has happened. My spirit is fine, Father. It's my body that has been assaulted, so it's my body that is crying out now in pain, in weariness, in unbelief.*

You know, better than anyone else, how human I am. You know how I've always tried to take care of myself, how healthy I've always been. You know how I've kept myself in shape and tried to stay attractive. My motives have been good for the most part—I believe You want your children to stay fit and healthy. And I wanted to be beautiful to Jim.

But maybe I have misused what You've given me and been too proud of the way I looked, too interested in my appearance, too concerned about the way I looked to other people, even other men, and not enough about the way I looked to You.

But we've been through all this before, haven't we God? You know how I am—You made me! And You have been able to use me, just the way I am, when I've let You. Only You and I know in what ways and how often I've failed You, displeased You, shamed You.

My body cries now because of the mutilation, the deformity it must learn to accept. It hurts—it hurts so much deep inside me where no one can see but You.

The smiling, optimistic me that everyone sees is not a false front, God. I am joyful, grateful, and filled to overflowing with Your love. But it's hard, Father, to hold my head up when my pride has been so wounded. I'm embarrassed, too. I'll get over that, I know, or at least learn to live with it better. But today, for now, it's rough.

So please excuse me while I cry. I know You are here; I know You care. But I don't want Your comfort right now. I just want to cry.

As the heavy flow of tears cascaded down my face, I tried to muffle the sound of my sobbing in my pillow. Restraint was impossible; self-control was gone. I was lost in the depths of despair, darkness, and dread that had been growing steadily within me. Like a cleansing stream, my tears were flowing from deep within, purging me of the dark thoughts, the fears, the self-pity.

I cried because of the things I knew; I cried because of things I didn't know. The immediate future was going to be so difficult for me because I would be so incapacitated, so dependent on others, and the thought was dreadful to me. Already I had been lying here for two weeks while others took care of my family, my chores, *me*. And I faced at least another month of being practically helpless.

O God! How can I stand it? I didn't know my pride was so great. Pride is nothing but self. Let me lose my self. Help me accept graciously the help others will offer me. O God! God! I can't stand being so helpless. I don't like it! Help me bear it. Let me learn this lesson. Let me learn to take and allow someone else the blessing of giving.

Gradually my thoughts were turned outward, away from myself, and my tears fell in torrents for the pain of those who loved me. I saw the situation from a different perspective, through *their* eyes, and their pain was worse than mine. I thought of Jim and the children. I thought especially of my parents and the agony they must have gone through during my surgery. How could I have borne it if it had been *my* child in that operating room all those hours? So many others came to mind—my in-laws, who loved me as a daughter, my brothers and my sister, other family, close friends, so many who cared, so many who shared this burden with me.

Oh, bless them, Father. Bless those who hurt because of me. Thank You for their love. Thank You for their expressions of love to me—for prayers and visits and love gifts. Thank You for the ones who have shown their love by caring for the children, helping with meals, doing the laundry. Be close to them all, Father. Give them Your peace.

By degrees, bit by bit, the flow of tears was slackening. The sobs subsided to sniffles. Feeling totally drained, almost devoid of feeling, I lay quietly savoring the peacefulness of the moment.

When I heard the door open I was slightly resentful. "Somebody can't read," I thought, disgusted. Turning my head toward the door I saw my visitor—Dr. Garrett.

"I guess you don't count," I said, glad to see him in spite of myself. "This is office hours—don't you ever work?"

He came around and sat beside me on the bed. "Having a rough day?" he asked gently.

I tried to explain. "I just needed to cry. It's no big deal. I'm okay."

"You *are* okay, you know. You're going to live to be a hundred. Is that what you're depressed about?"

"I'm not depressed! Am I the only one in the world who ever cries?" But my protests were feeble. I guess I was a little down and he knew it.

"Oh, Dr. Garrett," I said, my voice quivering. "You've really messed me up! I look so awful, and I'll always look this way. Today—just today—I can't cope with that. Tomorrow I'll be your model patient again."

I stopped to blow my nose, then continued. "In addition to that, I face over a month of cobalt treatments. That means daily trips to Lufkin, which means someone has to drive me, do my housework, keep my kids, cook my meals. Is that enough or shall I continue?"

"I understand how you feel, but it's all going to work out. Right now you've got to think about *you*. I don't want you worrying; your family loves you, and they'll manage. I just want you to rest and get your strength back. By midsummer this will be only a bad dream."

He continued to talk, comforting me, soothing my battered spirit, making me feel better just by being there. I wondered if the nurse had called him, but I didn't ask. It was enough to know he was there.

After a while I said, "Listen. I'm okay now. You don't have to worry about me. Thanks for babysitting. I'm sorry about falling apart like that."

Giving my hand a pat, he got up. "Don't feel bad about that. Now I know you're normal!"

He walked to the door and paused. "By the way," he said offhandedly, "I'm going to kick you out of here about Friday!"

Chapter Nine

Children of all ages have fears they often can't express, but as a mother, you know when something is troubling them. The fact that you have been in the hospital has caused them alarm. Explain it in terms you're sure they'll understand. Better than words are attitudes and actions. Show them you love them as you always have. Give them the chance to show their love for you. It's up to you to let them know that you are still very much their mother and you know how to do that in the warmest way possible.

Reach to Recovery
Terese Lasser

Children are the anchors that hold a mother to life.
Sophocles

Now no chastening for the present seemeth to be joyous, but grievous: nevertheless afterward it yieldeth the peaceable fruit of righteousness unto them which are exercised thereby.

Wherefore lift up the hands which hang down, and the feeble knees;

And make straight paths for your feet, lest that which is lame be turned out of the way; but let it rather be healed.

Hebrews 12:11-13

Conflicting emotions accompanied the announcement that I would soon be released from the hospital. On one hand I was eager to go, desperate to go, in hopes of returning some semblance of normalcy to my life as soon as possible. On the other hand, leaving the security and seclusion of my hospital room was frightening. I would have to pick up my life and start over, and my success would depend mainly on my attitude, my strength, and my ability to accept and cope with reality.

As the few remaining days in the hospital passed, I became alternately elated and depressed. With the elation came great resolutions: I would go home, do my exercises faithfully, take advantage of my convalescence by reading to the children, visiting with friends, writing letters; I would make the world's speediest recovery, physically and mentally, and be the best-adjusted one-breasted woman alive!

Then my "alter ego" intruded upon my plan making, bringing gloomy thoughts and making me want to do nothing so much as hide in the bathroom and never come out. Who was I kidding, anyway? My back hurt so much I could hardly find ease in any position. How was I going to tolerate *Jim* in my bed, much less the children? Talking to visitors was fine, but would I be able to enjoy it lying there like a circus sideshow freak while they paraded in and out to see me? How could I endure the inactivity? I'd go crazy and take everybody else with me!

Somehow, knowing I would be coming back to the hospital every day for five weeks was comforting. In two weeks' time I had come to depend on the doctors and nurses, confident that if some vague, undefined "something" went wrong they would be right there to handle it. Leaving them would be traumatic! Is this how a baby feels when it's weaned from bottle or breast, or has its security blanket taken away?

Dr. Garrett removed my pancake on Thursday, pulling the tubes out as gently as possible. Almost all the drainage had stopped, and I was glad; I didn't want to go home still hooked up to the Hemo-Vac. But, cumbersome as that apparatus was, I had become accustomed (attached?) to it. My dismissal from the hospital became a reality when that funny-looking little pancake and I parted company.

Thursday night before I got ready for bed I began preparations for going home. I threw away some wilted flowers, took the cards off the wall, and gathered up the belongings that filled the room and made it personally mine. I tired very quickly. This brief activity told me more than the doctor ever could about my condition and the importance of rest; the weakness was unbelievable. I would have no choice but to take it easy.

It was difficult to sleep that night. I picked up the little booklet Laura had made for me and glanced through it, pausing to admire the pictures of my family. There was Jim, serious-faced, sitting behind his tax office desk at school. Such a good man, a good husband—what kind of wife would I be to him now?

The pictures of herself and Ross that Laura had chosen were taken in our old Diboll home. Both kids were wearing clothes I had made for them—Ross a beige leisure suit, and Laura a red knit dress with white piping trim and a big white buckle that had come from her granddaddy Nethery's store. How long would it be before I could sew for them again?

Rick's picture was taken in front of the "little house" where we had lived those seemingly endless months while building the new house. His striped overalls and straw hat made him look like the little country boy that he was now. Just below his photo was one of Lana. She had just learned to crawl at the time, and the camera caught her expression of wonder and eagerness to explore that came with her new ability to get where she wanted to go. How could these two little ones understand why I couldn't pick them up? How long would it take me to undo all the spoiling well-meaning grandmothers and aunts would do?

Turning the pages I saw the signatures of the people who had visited me. Every name listed was special. Each one had contributed to the feeling of love that had enveloped me throughout my confinement. The very first signature was that of Amy, my second-grade niece. Jeannie had brought Amy and Greg, who was six, to see me the night I checked into the hospital, and they had visited me frequently since. There was Greg's name, two inches tall, with the capital "G" printed backwards. They were special to me and, although I had enjoyed their frequent visits, seeing their names here reminded me that I wouldn't be able to have them stay with us as often as I'd planned this summer.

I would miss Jeannie. She had come faithfully to visit every day on her lunch hour and often at night. She felt frustrated because her job kept her from helping more with the children, but she was making plans to keep all of them during her two-week vacation in July.

I looked at the page that held the names of the G.A. girls (a mission-focused girls' group from the Diboll church), who had come Wednesday night during prayer meeting time. I had taught these girls for years, in G.A. and in Church Training on Sunday nights. Seeing them again was a real joy. Jeannie was teaching them now, and it had been her idea to bring them last night.

I saw Joanna's name and recalled all the good times we'd had talking during the past two weeks. A close friend from Diboll days, Joanna and I shared one special common interest: end-times prophecy. Every letter or phone call that passed between us contained some reference to the subject, and whenever we were together we shared newly discovered tidbits from the Bible or current events from the newspapers relating to the second coming of Christ.

Two other visitors' names caught my attention. The first one, Faye, was a sister of Rick and Lana's "real" mother; the second name, that of their "real" grandmother. Faye had been almost like a sister to me ever since I'd met her, shortly after Lana's birth. She had helped us in our struggle to provide a permanent home for her little niece and nephew, and she had been a frequent and welcome visitor these past weeks. Her mother had been to see me also, expressing her love for me and all my family. The relationship between these two women and me is precious and quite unique. They were willing to relinquish all claims and rights to the children to insure that Rick and Lana had a real home and abundant love and security. Both insist on being known to the children only as "Mommy's friends," and they never intrude in our lives. Although infrequently, both have been in our home, and I make it a point to send snapshots of the children to their "backstage" grandmother, hoping in some small way to ease her pain in having lost them due to unpleasant and uncontrollable circumstances.

Slowly closing the book, I thought again how fortunate I was to have so many people who cared about me. I knew they all hoped and prayed I would have a complete recovery. I couldn't let them down. I would draw on their strength, count on their prayers, and accept gratefully their offers to help.

The sleeping pill the nurse had given me earlier was beginning to take effect. I switched out the overhead light and silently sent an earnest plea heavenward: *Please, Father, help me tomorrow. I want to go home more than anything in the world, but I'm afraid. The fear is so silly, so unreasonable; yet it is very real. Give me courage to face life again. Give me strength to recover, hope for the future, a happy heart.*

And please, please, wrap Your love around me like a shield to keep depression from finding a place to enter. I will be so vulnerable, so weak. I know where the devil will attack, so help me be strong and and on guard.

Immediately a Bible verse, 1 John 4:4, came to mind: "Greater is he that is in you, than he that is in the world." With that comforting thought I drifted calmly into sleep.

*   *   *

By the time Jim and Mama arrived to take me home, I had already had a full morning. It began with Bonnie, my nurse's aide friend, waking me up to say "good-bye" before she went off duty at 7:00. One by one the day shift nurses came in to wish me well. Dr. Garrett and Dr. Connell both made morning calls, complete with instructions, prescriptions for pain pills and sleeping pills, and cheerful farewells.

Dr. Connell told me to call her office and make an appointment for a breast check, pelvic, and pap smear in six months. Dr. Garrett made more extensive demands:

"I won't need to see you while you're getting the cobalt treatments. Dr. Kistler will be looking after you. But I'll want to see you once a month for the first year following surgery, then every three months the next year. And I want you to call if you have any problems. Okay?"

"Don't worry! I'll call," I stated firmly. Then, suspiciously, "Is there any particular problem I should look for?"

"Not especially. If you take care of yourself I don't expect any difficulties at all. But if you start trying to do your housework or lift those babies, you'll set yourself back and make your convalescence that much longer. You may not notice at first that you're overdoing it, but months from now you'll be coming to me complaining of all sorts of vague symptoms fatigue, headaches, pain, depression—and it will be because you haven't done what I said. I've seen it happen time and again." The twinkle in his eye belied the sternness of the admonishment.

"Yes, sir!" I replied, pretending to be cowed by the harshness of his words. "Whatever you say, sir. Just don't hit me!"

He grinned. "I *am* serious, though. It's important that you take care of yourself."

"Okay, I understand that, but you don't know what you're asking. We can't afford to hire any help. Our financial situation was bleak *before* all this. Now it's going to be desperate! I'm not the sit-down-and-be-lazy type, anyway. I'm within a stone's throw of being a perfectionist, in fact, and I'm cursed with an overdose of efficiency. I *have* to do things. I have to do them *right*.

And I have to do them right *now*. How am I going to change my whole personality?"

"Don't. Just let it lie dormant for about a month. If you'll take a strict rest, at least until the cobalt treatments are over, you can begin to resume normal activities slowly and soon be back to top performance level. Look at it this way: This is a chance of a lifetime, lying around being waited on! Relax and enjoy it!"

But I knew I couldn't. I might obey his orders, but I wouldn't enjoy it. Not when I knew everybody else was going to have to double up on his or her work load to take up the slack in mine.

*   *   *

A few short hours later I was headed home, propped up on pillows thoughtfully brought along by Jim, surrounded by plants and people I loved. Mama and Lana were in the back seat. Lana had been at Linda's for the previous few days, and I was delighted to have her back with me so soon. I could hardly wait to have the whole family all together in one place again.

The drive home was pleasant. Everything seemed new to me after having been indoors for so long. I was hungry for the sight of trees and sunshine and blue skies, and so eager to see my home. Finally, after what seemed ages, Jim turned into our drive that wound up a hill, through a lane overhung with trees. And there it was! Home! The first sight of it thrilled me and gave me a boost that no medicine in the world could have provided. Set back among the trees on the sloping hillside, like a diamond in a rare gold setting, the house nestled comfortably, looking for all the world as if it had *grown* there. Tall, serene, quiet, it welcomed me.

The peace was short-lived! As soon as Jim stopped the car, children and dogs came running from every direction. Hugging and kissing and dog licks intermingled with squeals of joy, laughter, and shouts of "Mommy, Mommy!"

I was home!

Laura had prepared signs and banners that proclaimed: "Welcome home, Mom." Bernice had fixed a delicious meal, keeping strictly within the bounds of the bland diet Dr. Garrett had ordered for me for a while. The house was cool and clean, and the sheets on my bed were freshly laundered and inviting. Everything had been done to make my homecoming delightful.

I had insisted that all the children be at home. Nobody but me thought this was a good idea, and probably it *was* unwise strictly from the standpoint of my getting plenty of rest. Yet, I had missed them so much, and it seemed to me that their welfare had to be considered, too. They needed to be with me, to see that I was okay and at home where I belonged. Then, after several days, when their security was re-established, they would be eager once again to visit this aunt or that one and not feel anxiety. Mommy would be home waiting for them.

In spite of wanting to be with them, though, I was thankful when they were finally down for afternoon naps. I, too, went to bed, almost completely exhausted from the slight exertion of the trip home. I took two Darvon capsules for the pain in my back, which never seemed to let up, and lay down with a hot water bottle under my aching left shoulder blade. I had asked for a hot water bottle in the hospital but was informed they didn't have one. Now I almost cried with pleasure as the delicious warmth crept through my back, easing the pain that had been my constant companion since surgery. Soon I was asleep—in my own bed, in my own home once again. Blessed, wonderful joy!

*   *   *

"Mommy? Are you awake?"

Through the fog of my drugged sleep I heard Laura's voice. *What is she doing here at the hospital?* I opened my eyes. *No! It's not the hospital. I'm home!*

"I'm awake, honey. Come on in." I carefully pulled the covers up over my thin nightgown. I wasn't sure just how much and how soon to show my daughter the extent of the surgery's effect. Laura and I were close, and mother-daughter talks were common and frequent. I would not try to hide anything from her; I had already decided that. But I needed to wait for the right time. I tried to sense her mood as she sat down beside me.

Anxiously she asked, "Are you okay? Do you need anything?" Worry. Concern. *What can I do to help her?* Thinking rapidly, I came to the obvious conclusion: *Of course! It will help her to help me!*

"I sure am glad you came in just now. I need some hot water in this thing." I rolled over on my good side so that she could reach the water bottle. I explained to her how to fill it and "burp" the air out.

"That feels so good. Thank you," I said when she returned. "You'll just have to be my new nurse. I'm going to need some help with my exercises, too."

Her eyes lit up. "I'll be right back," she promised mysteriously. In a few minutes she returned with a little table and a cowbell.

"I'm going to put this right here by your bed. Whenever you need me, you just ring the bell!"

"Now that is a great idea," I exclaimed. "I never would have thought of that!"

She sat down again. "Do you need anything else?"

"Just to talk to you. Tell me all about the recital tonight. Are you ready?"

"I think so. I wish you could go."

"I do, too. I could just cry thinking about missing it. But Daddy is going to take the tape recorder and the camera, so I'll get to see you and hear you later. Tell you what. Go plug in my hot rollers, and I'll help you fix your hair!" I wasn't sure how I would manage that, but I had to do something to be a part of this important night. For Laura. And for me.

While I struggled to get the rollers in place, Laura chatted happily about the duets and trios she and Ross would be playing in addition to their two solos. I bit my lips to hide the pain of lifting my left arm. I tried to convince myself that this was not *work*; it was *therapy*. Soon her shoulder-length hair had a bouncy curl on the ends.

Gratefully sinking back onto the bed, I said with as much enthusiasm as I could muster, "Now hand me that white paper sack, and I'll show you what we have to do."

She listened eagerly while I explained the various exercises and the ways she could help me. The idea of being my nurse and therapist was exciting; she could hardly wait to begin.

"Wait a minute," I pleaded. "Let's start on this in the morning. I'm too tired today. But starting tomorrow, I want you to make me do these exercises twice a day, no matter what!"

Inspired by her newly acquired importance to Mommy, she practically danced out of the room. I waited a few minutes and then rang the cowbell fiercely.

"Nurse Nethery, Nurse Nethery," I called loudly. Breathlessly she bounded up the stairs and into my room. Stopping just short of being in bed with me, she struggled to regain her composure.

"May I help you?" she asked politely.

"Yes," I replied. "I need a kiss."

*   *   *

I awoke early the next morning, accustomed to hospital routine. No one else was awake. The quiet was beautiful; the only sounds I heard atop our country hillside were those of the birds welcoming the day.

I shifted my weight cautiously, unwilling to wake either Jim or the pain, both of which were resting peacefully. I lifted my head slowly to peer over the pillow that separated us and protected my chest from a flying elbow or arm during the night. I had found that, even when I was alone, a soft pillow over my chest made me feel more comfortable. The idea of anything touching me there was unbearable; I couldn't even touch myself without flinching.

Around eight o'clock I heard the garage door open. I knew it was Bernice coming to begin breakfast preparations and corral the kids when they got up. Without consulting me, she and my mother had decided on a plan for my month of convalescence. They would alternate days, one taking care of the children, house, and meals one day, the other the next.

Jim and I were helpless to object; what choice did we have? He had to work, and I couldn't work. But both of us vowed to make it as easy on them as possible. When Jim was home, he would take over the babysitting. With some encouragement and instructions from me, Laura could assume many more responsibilities around the house. Ross had a pretty full schedule of lawnmowing commitments, but he, too, could be counted on to take an additional chore or two.

"Together we'll make it," I thought. "We are a family, and this is a family affair. We love each other, and there's no sacrifice any of us would not make for another. This is the way God intended a family to function, and all our years of loving and training and growing together have prepared us for handling a crisis such as this."

I tried unsuccessfully to go back to sleep. I was not too disappointed that I couldn't, for I knew that any minute now one of the little ones would be up and heading for our bed. I looked forward to it. It had been a long time since all six of us had piled into our king-sized bed for a Saturday morning get-together.

I didn't have long to wait. I heard the little footsteps just a few seconds before I saw the pony-tailed head of 20-month-old Lana peeking in. With a grin from ear to ear she ran to the bedside, struggling to swing a short little leg up over the side. I reached down cautiously with my right arm, placed a hand under the thick padding of double diapers, rubber pants, and pajama bottoms, and gave her the boost she needed.

"You came home?" she asked, as she snuggled up close, clutching her "bankie," the blue quilted blanket I'd made for her before she even came home from the hospital.

"Mommy came home. And Mommy loves Lana." I gave her a kiss, hoping she'd be still and let me cuddle her for a little while. I should have known better. Lana was a whirlwind of activity. Her vocabulary was enormous, and she had been talking in sentences since she was a year old. Her speech seemed incongruous with her diminutive size; people were always commenting, amazed, "She can *talk*?"

Now she wanted to get in my "bathtub." Last night, while Jim and the older kids were gone to the recital, Lana and Rick, with Mama riding herd, had played on my bed awhile. Lana had wriggled herself into a position between my legs which, covered as they were with the bed clothes, reminded her somehow of a bathtub. She played there happily for a long time; and many times in the coming weeks "Mommy's bathtub" was a favorite place to be.

Jim was awake, too, when Rick joined us, his big brown eyes even brighter at finding Mommy still home. When Grandmommy came upstairs to investigate the voices, she was horrified to find the kids in bed with me, certain they would fall on me or hurt me in some way. Secretly, I was worried about the same possibilities. It was a relief when they were taken down to breakfast!

Later Grandmommy took the two little ones down the hill to her house for a while, and Laura and I began our exercise session. Jim and Ross sat on the bed, eager to see what was going to happen. I would discover, as weeks went by, that having an audience gave me more incentive; I always accomplished more when someone was there to encourage and applaud.

At my request, Laura brought some chalk from her room. "I want you to mark on the door how high I can reach today. Each day I'll try to reach higher, and the marks will show us what kind of progress I'm making."

Dutifully Laura positioned herself beside me, chalk ready, as I placed my fingers chest high on the closet door and began "walking" them upwards. Slowly they crept up—shoulder level, chin level, eye level! I stopped, unable to move another quarter-inch.

"Come on, Mom," Laura urged. "Just a little bit more."

Determined not to disappoint her, I tried again. Almost imperceptibly my fingers moved higher. Encouraged, I kept trying. Sweat broke out on my forehead; my arm felt as if it weighed a hundred pounds. Finally my fingers reached a point some inches above my head.

"That's it. That's all I can do," I gasped.

Jim and Ross clapped their hands in appreciation. I gave a slight bow, acknowledging their approval, and quickly sat down. Ross was astonished that I was so incapacitated. I explained about the missing muscle that connected my arm to my chest and how different muscles would have to be trained to compensate.

"Will you ever be back to normal?" he asked anxiously.

"Listen, boy! In another month I'll be tearing you up on the basketball court again," I said with conviction.

"You wish!" he retorted, grinning.

Hoping I'd convinced him, I picked up the red ball with the elastic string attached and placed the loop on my middle finger.

"Okay now, folks. Keep your eye on the bouncing rubber ball. I'm going to throw it. It will come back to me. I probably won't catch it, but that doesn't matter. It's the throwing and the reaching that count!"

I threw the ball outward with as much strength as I could. The elastic stretched, snapped back, and returned the ball forcibly to hit my wounded chest.

"Oh!" I screamed, instinctively reaching to protect my chest, a useless gesture now that the damage was done. Jim tried to keep a straight face, in deference to my pain, but failed miserably and doubled up with laughter.

"Hey, that's a neat exercise," Ross said. "Let's see that one again!"

Even Laura laughed when she saw that I wasn't seriously hurt.

Exasperated, I said, "There's got to be a better way." Maybe

Terese Lasser didn't have anybody to play ball *with* or maybe she wore a chest protector.

I picked the ball up again, pulled the elastic off, and stood beside the bed. "You stand over there by Daddy's desk, Ross. You can help with this exercise."

When we were both in position, I said, "I'll throw the ball to you, underhand at first, and you throw it back." Confidently, I threw the ball. It landed on the bed about two feet away, and again I clutched my shoulder, moaning in agony.

In frustration I picked the ball up with my right hand, placed it in my left hand, and tried again. This time I was more cautious. *Slowly* I drew my arm back and brought it forward, releasing the ball in one smooth motion. This time it reached Ross. Again the applause from the onlookers. Encouraged, we played pitch, such as it was, for several minutes.

"Okay, Laura. One more, and that's all I can take for a while. Bring that piece of rope, and let's go to your bathroom."

Everybody trooped into the children's bath. I straddled the tub and instructed Laura to loop the rope over the shower rod above. I grasped a tongue-depressor handle in each hand and pulled carefully down with my right hand. The left arm rose slowly. I tried to establish a slow "see-saw" movement, pulling the left hand higher each time. The tightness through my chest and my inability to stretch the arm any higher was discouraging. I, too, wondered if I'd ever be back to normal.

I was tired. "Okay, the show's over. Just toss your money on the bed before you leave."

Laura put away all the equipment and drew my bath water. I took a long, hot bath, still avoiding water on my incision, and then rubbed lotion all over my tired body. I put on a fresh gown, some makeup, and combed my hair; then I crawled wearily back into bed.

This routine—breakfast, exercise, bath, bed, lunch, nap, exercise, bed, supper, bedtime—soon became an established procedure. Interspersed with these activities were letter writing, reading, visiting with people who came to see me, and talking to the kids. Several ladies brought food they had prepared, and I was so grateful. Each dish meant less work for the two mothers.

Each day I made a little more progress with my arm; each day I felt a little stronger. My cobalt treatments were supposed to begin in about two weeks. I felt that by that time I would be feeling good and ready to begin the ordeal of daily trips to Lufkin.

Tuesday, June 1, four days after I came home from the hospital, the phone rang. Mama answered and called up the stairs, "Susan, it's for you."

I reached for the phone beside me. "Hello?"

"Mrs. Nethery? This is Jean Dixon at the Kurth Radiation Center. We're ready to begin your treatments. Can you come tomorrow morning, about ten o'clock?"

Chapter Ten

The single biggest psychological adjustment a woman must make is to the sudden knowledge that she has a chronic, potentially fatal disease and that removing the breast is only the first step in trying to stop the malignant spread.

Breast Cancer, a Personal History and an Investigative Report
Rose Kushner

Adversity is the path of truth.
Lord Byron

Though our outward man perish, yet the inward man is renewed day by day.

For our light affliction, which is but for a moment, worketh for us a far more exceeding and eternal weight of glory;

While we look not at the things which are seen, but at the things which are not seen: for the things which are seen are temporal; but the things which are not seen are eternal.

2 Corinthians 4:16-18

At 9:30 the next morning, Jim and I were sitting in the radiation center reception room. The morning had been hectic; I was already tired and I hadn't even had my treatment. Not knowing what to expect made me tense and apprehensive. The waiting made it worse.

"Can you believe," I said to Jim wearily, "that just two weeks ago today I was in this hospital having a *mastectomy?*"

"I couldn't tell by looking," he replied, smiling.

I was grateful for the compliment. Vanity's name being woman, I had worried about getting out in public before I could wear a bra. Because of this, I had spent several hours after Mrs. Dixon's call trying to rig up some kind of underwear to hide my disfigurement. The end result of my ingenuity was strange looking, but effective.

Jim had donated an old T-shirt. I cut the sleeves out, shortened it, and cut it open down the front. (There was no way I could get it on over my head; besides, I knew I'd be taking it off and on for treatments so it needed to be easy to manage.) I took a bust dart in both sides to give it a little shape, then cut a circle from the discarded tail of the shirt. I sewed the circle inside, on the left, corresponding to the position of the right breast, and stuffed it loosely with fiberfill. Sewing snaps on the front completed the project, providing me with a loose-fitting, comfortable garment that gave me enough shape under gathered tops and nightgowns so that I looked almost normal! I was pleased with the result and planned to make several more; I knew I would not be able to wear a bra until the treatments were over, and possibly not for weeks after that.

Finding clothes to wear had already proved to be a major problem. (I would find this to be true even months later when I had my prosthesis.) For the first time in my life I could truthfully say, "I don't have a thing to wear."

None of my "before" clothes met the necessary requirements. Anything I wore now had to be loose (to hide the fact that I only needed half a bra and wasn't wearing even that), button-front (because of impaired arm movements, nothing could go on over my head, and I couldn't manage anything that closed behind), and high-necked (the flesh had been carved out of my chest almost up to my collarbone, making it almost impossible to wear even a moderately scooped-out neckline.) I did not have one single garment that incorporated all those features!

The day after I had discovered this awful fact, Jim surprised me by taking home an armload of blouses for me to try on! Several he had brought "worked" and, paired with my own jeans and pants, made comfortable, attractive outfits. I was wearing one of these tops today, and I was certain that, without detailed scrutiny, "only my surgeon knew for sure."

Finally, after what seemed hours (but really wasn't long), an attractive woman about my age came out into the waiting area, introduced herself as Jean Dixon, and asked me to come with her. We went through a small room containing desks, files, etc., and into a larger room guarded by a red light (when the machine was in operation) and signs marked "Danger–Radiation," or something similar. Inside I saw a mammoth piece of machinery dwarfing the bed that was rolled under it.

"This is 'Big Bertha,' " Mrs. Dixon said, "and by the way, you can call me Jean."

Jean and I soon established a rapport that was to remain throughout the treatment period and beyond. Her consideration and interest in me put me at ease immediately. We soon found common interests: both of us were Baptists; we were the same age (32); we were both avid readers.

She was amazed at the underwear I had fashioned. "That is really unique," she said, "and the cotton material is exactly what you are supposed to wear over the incision during the weeks of your treatment! How did you know?"

"I didn't know. I just did the first thing that came to mind." Silently I thanked God for His direction in even this small matter.

"Do you mind if I call the other girl in here to see this?" Jean asked.

"Of course not," I replied. "I always wanted to model underwear!"

"The other girl" was Florence Green, who worked in this department with Jean. She was younger, with long, straight blond hair and a soft voice and eyes. She, too, was surprised at my "invention," commenting that most women who came for treatments wore big coats or sweaters to hide their surgery or else just came "flat."

"Maybe they aren't as young as I am," I said, "or not as vain!"

"Not as creative, most likely," Jean proposed. "*I* wouldn't have thought of that."

I lay down on the table and was covered with a sheet. They

explained what they were going to do while we waited for Dr. Kistler to come in.

Turning on the machine's light above me, Jean showed me how the light indicated the area covered by radiation. "However," she explained, "we won't need to treat that large a place, so we'll use these lead bricks to block the rays from reaching anyplace except where Dr. Kistler specifies."

She placed one of the lead blocks in my hand. It was very heavy. "Please don't drop that on me," I pleaded, horrified at the thought.

"We haven't lost *too* many patients that way," she revealed reassuringly.

We were laughing when Dr. Kistler entered. "Can I join the party?" he asked. Shaking my hand, he inquired about my progress and began to examine me.

"It's not pretty, is it?" I said, referring to the still raw incision and the overall ugliness of the cavity that once was my left breast.

"I think it looks good," he protested, speaking from a medical point of view. "Dr. Garrett did a great job. Now some I've seen—" He left the sentence unfinished, causing me to speculate on how it could possibly be worse. Nevertheless, I agreed that my scar was healing nicely; the incision had been smooth and clean, and I knew Dr. Garrett had worked hard to sew me back together without having to use a skin graft from my legs or back. I appreciated his endeavors. But it was still ugly!

Dr. Kistler explained again why they felt radiation was called for in my case, informed me that I would have twenty-five treatments of about five minutes duration each, and warned me of possible side effects of nausea, tenderness of the treated area, and weakness. Periodically I would be given blood tests to ascertain whether or not the treatments should be discontinued for a day or two (something about the white blood count).

As he talked, he positioned the lead blocks on the plastic shelf above me, blocking out the light until he had formed a rough "L" shape, several inches wide, with the remaining light. The "L" was inverted with the short leg going from my arm across the collarbone to my neck and the long leg going from my neck down the left side of the chest, stopping where my scar did at the bottom of my rib cage.

"Okay. It's ready to mark," he said to Jean. "See you in a few days, or sooner if you have a problem."

When he had gone, Jean got a little jar of red fluid and began to paint on my skin a dotted outline of the area to be treated. "This is permanent ink, so don't worry about it when you're bathing. We do this so we won't have to go through the 'positioning' procedure each day. With the outline we can get the radiation on the exact spot Dr. Kistler originally indicated.

"Permanent?" I managed to ask weakly, imagining myself going through life with an "L"-shaped tattoo on my chest.

"Just for a few weeks," Jean laughed. "In fact, we'll have to retouch it a few times during the five weeks, I'm sure. Okay. I think we're ready. You just lie perfectly still. I'll be right outside, sitting where I can see you through that little window." She pointed to it. "And there's an intercom system so I can hear you if you call."

It took just a few minutes after they had left the room to close the doors and set the machine. Then I heard the rumble of the motor switching on. I felt absolutely nothing. Before I knew it, the treatment was over; I was dressed and back in the car with Jim.

"That wasn't bad at all," I told him. "Hardly seems worth

driving to Lufkin for just that short length of time."

I explained the whole procedure as we drove home, even reading aloud the little booklet on radiation therapy they had given me. I was especially interested in a white slip of paper entitled, "Instruction to Patients Treated by X-Rays or Radium":

Some redness and tenderness of the skin is to be expected about two or three weeks after beginning treatment.

It is important to observe the following instructions in order to keep the skin healthy and avoid trouble now or in the future:

1. Keep the area dry.
2. Do not wash the part treated, except with clear water (no soap).
3. Do not apply ointments or lotions (unless prescribed by the doctor).
4. Do not apply heat in any form, either during treatment or afterwards.
5. Avoid direct sunshine or cold on part treated.
6. Wear cotton clothing *only* next to treated areas.
7. Do not skip or miss treatments. Notify Doctor if this happens.

"Isn't that a coincidence," I pointed out. "About the cotton clothing, I mean?"

*　　*　　*

On the way through Lufkin we stopped at a business supply store and purchased a large journal. I had commented earlier that I'd like to keep some kind of diary during the coming months to give me something different to do and provide a record of our home life for the children to read when they grew up. In my heart I had an additional reason: I knew the first year following breast cancer surgery was critical. If I died, I wanted to leave something of myself behind for the kids—some of my thoughts, written proof of my love, a diary of family activities. I promised myself that I would keep it faithfully for a year; I made my first entry the day of my first cobalt treatment.

June 2, 1976

Cancer is *always* something that happens to someone else. So are cobalt treatments. But just two weeks ago today I had surgery for cancer, and today I took the first of many cobalt treatments! Unbelievable!

I am calm and peaceful inside. Maybe I haven't fully realized yet what has happened to me, and someday soon it will hit me: "O my God! *Cancer!*" But I don't think that will happen. I believe that the peace I feel is the peace of God as promised in two of my favorite Bible passages: Philippians 4:6 (And the peace of God, which passeth all understanding, shall keep your hearts and minds through Christ Jesus) and Matthew 11: 29 (And ye shall find rest unto your souls).

My attitude is one of praise and joy. This is not my natural attitude, for it is not by nature a human attitude. It comes from God's Holy Spirit as a special gift to me to keep me from falling victim to depression, self-pity, and despair. So many prayers have been lifted in my behalf; because of them, and because I am a child whom God loves, I am perhaps more a "whole woman" than I was before part of my body was cut away.

I am so thankful the cancerous lump was discovered in time. I am alive! God loves me; my family and friends love and care for me; and I'm the luckiest woman in the world. No, not luckiest—most blessed.

I'm very tired tonight. The trip to Lufkin for the treatment was long, and I've had lots of company since I returned home. The two babies are asleep, and Jim, Ross, and Laura are watching a ball game on T.V. There's so much I want to write, but I've got to get some sleep.

*   *   *

Because of the daily trips to Lufkin, the "mothers" had to take on double duty. On the days they weren't keeping house and kids, they usually had to drive me to get my treatments. Other people helped—friends, relatives (Jim and Papa took me when they could)—but the burden of transporting me fell mainly to Mama and Bernice.

For a brief time the daily excursions were pleasant. The long drive allowed time for conversation that was hardly possible under ordinary circumstances; and, on the occasions that someone other than the immediate family took me, the journey provided a chance to make, or strengthen, friendships. The people at the radiation center were all so nice. The two other doctors there, Dr. Seitz and Dr. Shelton, were as kind and sensitive as Dr. Kistler. All three of them were always cheerful and smiling.

On the days when I had to go to the lab on the second floor, I'd swing around and say "hello" to my nurses on Henderson Wing. They never failed to boost my spirits and make me feel beautiful!

However, I soon began to feel the effects of the radiation and came to dread the trips immensely. I almost hated to go to bed, tired as I was, because it seemed that as soon as I did it was time to get up and go to Lufkin again. Writing in my journal during this painful period became my outlet. In addition to full pages each day devoted to family activities, personal feelings I might not otherwise express found release. I found a comfort through venting my emotions, both good and bad, in this way.

June 4

Saw Dr. Garrett at the hospital today end he told me I wasn't getting enough rest (after I told him my back hurt a lot and I wasn't sleeping well). Not enough rest! I'm in bed so much of the time people walk in and think I'm a pillow.

Jim has been so great through all this. He calls me his "unicorn" and doesn't seem to mind that I'm lopsided. He's great. To him, I'm still beautiful.

Rick is mad at Dr. Garrett and threatens to "cut that doctor" when he sees him! He can't imagine someone hurting Mommy even though I've assured him the doctor was helping me. It's hard to argue with such an awful scar.

June 6

We are looking forward to our first summer in our wonderful new home. Last summer in the "little house" was hardly heaven. We sure saved a lot of money doing so much on this one ourselves, but I almost ruined my health. I wonder how much importance *stress* plays as a key factor in cancer?

June 7

Right now Jim and the kids are down at Bernice's eating supper. I cannot seem to get over feeling guilty about accepting so much help from everyone. I'd much rather do it myself.

June 8

I've started a portrait of a young Indian girl. I saw her picture in a book (she was originally photographed by Curtis in the early 1900s) and it has haunted me ever since. Hope I can capture her. I've been eager to try and am just now feeling a little like it.

June 10

I painted Mosa's face today (my Indian girl) and it's coming so easy. She is so sad. Why? Everyone will have to decide for himself. She is my bicentennial contribution to America's past. She is America 1900, crying, perhaps, because her world has fallen apart. Do I have the same kind of tears in my eyes?

June 11

Today began like most days—trip to Lufkin for cobalt treatment. Seventeen more to go! Mama took me today. Bernice fixed supper and cleaned up the kitchen. If I were her "blood daughter" she could not treat me any better. She is so good to me and I am thankful for her love.

June 13

I had planned to go to church this morning, but I woke up with a pain in my stomach, or abdomen, or somewhere! I couldn't even get up to find Jim (who was outside) or even reach over to the phone to call Bernice. After about fifteen minutes it passed, but I haven't wanted to get out of bed all day.

Then, too, I'm having some difficulty swallowing. Feels like something's stuck in my throat. This is the first day since surgery that I've had the slightest hint of depression. I *refuse* to have it! I know that God and I together can handle it. Knowing that depression is my worst enemy at least prepares me for it. I know what to pray for protection *from*.

June 14

Dr. Shelton had to see me this morning. He said the lump in my throat was caused by the cobalt—a rare side effect and not one usually seen, if at all, till later in the treatments.

I haven't worked on Mosa in several days. I just haven't felt well enough. She'll wait for me.

Laura and I were having one of our heart-to-hearts this

afternoon. I was telling her about how I pray each day that God will protect us from harm and evil. She said, "I pray for this house a lot—you know, that it won't burn. I told God if this house were alive it would be a Christian." Isn't that beautiful?

June 15

The rain started about 4:30 this morning, I guess, but we didn't realize it was such a heavy one till we got up. The whole entry hall, playroom, garage, half bath, and closets were an inch deep in water. What a mess! Mama was on her way over, it being her day, but I had to call Bernice to help, too. I hated to leave them with such a awful job.

Papa took me to Lufkin. He couldn't drive today with his Driver's Ed. kids because of the rain, so he was free to take me. I had to wait a long time—it was crowded today. Had to get another blood test. Also got a prescription from Dr. Seitz for "cobalt sunburn." Maybe I'll sleep better tonight.

June 18

Today we received an envelope, anonymously, with $500 cash in it. We were stunned, to say the least.

And yet, just two days ago, when we got the doctor's bill and found out that the insurance only paid $200, I asked the Lord to help us meet this need. Of course, I cried and carried on like a baby awhile *first*—just couldn't *think* how we'd pay that bill. It was all my fault, and the hospital bill hadn't even come in yet. But then I calmed down and remembered God's promises to meet our needs. I claimed that promise. He never fails. Has never yet. I love Him so. I have been so blessed through all this ordeal.

June 20

Jim and I didn't wake up until 9 o'clock! It was a rush around here to get off by 9:40. They made it. I got ready and went just to church. It was my first time since surgery.

I wore a beige-colored belted dress that was loose fitting and a leisure bra stuffed with fiberfill—didn't think it would hurt for just that hour. I even played the organ. Bernice has been playing the piano for me.

June 24

Woke up with a headache—third day in a row. Mama took me to Lufkin today. We saw Dr. Garrett in the hospital hall. He said I'm still not to do anything—not until the treatments are over.

June 25

I am still feeling so bad—nauseated, constipated, tired. Just eight more treatments!

Jim, Ross, and Laura worked out in the yard. Jim is so tired. It seems the work never ends when you build a house. I'm angry (or frustrated) because I can't get out and help him.

June 26

Jim and the kids have been working outside all day—raking newly bulldozed ground, loading and unloading all the rocks, planting grass seed, and watering. They are so tired.

I've been so frustrated all day wanting to get out there and help. How I'd have loved it! I consoled myself by painting. I think I've finished Mosa.

June 27

I didn't go to church this morning. I guess I'm just so tired by the time the week is over that I "give out" on the weekends. Can't rest well on Saturdays—things are so wild around here.

All of us are packing for trips tomorrow! I am going to spend a few days with the Weavers (our ex-pastor in Diboll). Ross is going to Jeannie's, and Laura is going with Bernice to Bryan to buy books and visit Pat. Lana is officially staying at Mama's, but Jim declares she will stay with him at night. Rick is at Jan's.

June 28-July 9

I'm writing this late. Went to Diboll to the Weaver's new home (parsonage) and got so involved in visiting, resting, getting treatments, etc., that I completely forgot about this journal!

Had such a lovely, restful time; I feel renewed, body and spirit, ready to start life all over again. My treatments are all over, thank goodness. The five weeks passed more quickly than I dreamed possible.

I got to Anita and Larry's about noon Monday after having my treatment. That was to turn out to be the only one that week until Friday night at eight o'clock! The machine broke down! Each day I waited for Jean to call and say it was fixed. I didn't want to go home and have to come right back. But I got a *much* needed rest and had a ball!

I went home early Saturday (with Jeannie and Ross) to the Halbert reunion at Mama's. There was a big crowd. Most people seemed a little embarrassed at seeing me. (My imagination?)

Stayed home till after dinner Sunday—had to be back in Lufkin at 3 o'clock for another treatment. (Jean came to the hospital through the weekend to make up for lost treatment days.) I just stayed with the Weavers through the rest of the week.

Finished my treatments Wednesday!

*   *   *

Washing dishes was fun! Making cornbread was fun! Doing the laundry was fun! Everything, even the most mundane task, took on an aura of enjoyment after I had been denied the pleasure of work for almost two months. Everywhere I looked, something needed to be done. And I could do it! Marvelous joy—to be able to do my own work again!

My "good-sense" self cautioned: "Don't overdo it. You're still not up to par." My "good-little-housewife" self countered: "But look what all needs to be done! Every drawer and closet in this house needs to be cleaned. Look at the windows! And the carpets—yuk—"

Striving to maintain a balance between the warring natures was difficult. Compromise was easier. I did strenuous jobs, such as thoroughly cleaning the kitchen; then I sat down and shelled butterbeans. Doing the ever-present laundry preceded a "sit-down" job such as catching up on the mending. I lay down on the couch to study my Sunday school lesson before tackling the dreaded job of cleaning the aquarium.

Somehow I survived, even thrived on this rigorous schedule. I knew the enchantment wouldn't last, but right now my housework had the same glory about it that it did when I was a newlywed and mopped the floors and dusted every day!

I continued to exercise my arm, although by Reach to Recovery standards it was back to normal. Not satisfied with merely being able to stretch my arm above my head, I lay down on the floor and strained to touch the floor with my arms outstretched above my head. This maneuver involved a few additional inches of "stretch," and I struggled for weeks before accomplishing this particular goal with ease and no pain.

Trying on clothes was one of the best exercises I "invented." It seemed to pull and hurt worse than any other, and that was my yardstick of the value of an exercise. If it hurt, it had to be good!

Ross and I had moved outside with our ball playing; I could throw the ball overhand and underhand for quite a distance and fairly accurately. (Considering I'm right-handed, that was quite an accomplishment!)

Resuming my daily walks to Cat Holler (my father-in-law's acreage behind our house) was one of my greatest pleasures. Before surgery, a three-mile walk was a normal, everyday occurrence. Aside from the enjoyment of being outside, alone, in the beautiful woods and pastureland, there was a large rock—big enough to sit on, perfect to kneel beside—that I called my altar. I told a cousin once: "God just sits on that rock and waits for me every day!" How I had missed the quiet and peace of my walks and the beauty of meeting God at my altar each day.

The days immediately following the conclusion of my cobalt treatments were almost heavenly. I felt as if I'd been reborn and each day was a new beginning. So euphoric, in fact, was my mood that I almost succeeded in blotting from my conscious thought the one thing that threatened to mar my bliss: the discovery of a small, brand new lump in my right breast.

Chapter Eleven

Any woman can develop breast cancer, but women with one or more of the following characteristics seem to be more *susceptible* to it than others. This does not mean that she is certain to develop breast cancer.

Women over 35, risk increases with age.

Women whose mothers or sisters have had breast cancer—risk is twice as high.

Women with history of benign breast disease.

Women who have experienced early onset of menstruation or have experienced late menopause.

Women who have never had a child.

Women who have one or two children are at a greater risk than women who have three or more children. (The risk goes down as the number of children increases.)

Women who have had a cancer in one breast.

Breast Cancer Fact Sheet
National Cancer Institute

No affliction would trouble a child of God, if he knew God's reason for sending it.

Morgan

Weeping may endure for a night, but joy cometh in the morning.

Psalm 30:5

The organ music was soothing, creating a mood of reverence before the sermon. Aunt B's accomplished fingers moved expertly over the keyboard; I had listened to her play that same organ in the same beautiful way since I was a child. She never had to look down at her feet to hit the correct foot pedal like I did when I played it! I guess that's one reason she's the organist and I'm the pianist!

I settled down to enjoy one of the few sermons I'd heard since my surgery. Our new pastor, Brother Manning Garrett, was just out of seminary. His messages were inspiring and well-prepared; I found his intellectual approach and his rapid-fire presentation stimulating. This morning, however, it was difficult to keep my thoughts on the preaching.

Jim and I were holding hands discreetly on our front row pew. I knew he was glad to have me back beside him. *Poor Jim. How can I tell him about the new lump I've found in my breast? How can I tell anybody? What is going on with me? Am I just "gun shy" now and imagining things?*

Two weeks ago I had discovered what I thought was a new lump. During one of my daily trips to Lufkin I had told Dr. Kistler and Dr. Garrett. Both had checked me and been unable to feel what I felt. Relieved, but still vaguely uneasy, I had accepted their opinions to a certain degree: I decided not to mention it to anyone else but would secretly keep a check on it. This morning, sitting quietly in church, I made the decision to tell Jim about it immediately after church. One very important reason prompted this decision: the lump had at least doubled in size.

To say I was not apprehensive would be lying. I knew if this lump were cancerous, that would mean that the original cancer had probably spread, possibly even to other parts of my body, and my prognosis would be poor. I found the idea frightening. Emotionally and physically I was weaker than I had ever been in my life. My moods were still swinging from lows to highs, and no matter how much rest I got I was still exhausted. The idea of a simple surgery was more than I could entertain; the possibility of more cancer was impossible to cope with.

As if through a haze, I heard Manning announce the scripture passage for that day: Romans 6. I knew how that chapter ended. It was a familiar verse that most children learn in Sunday school: "For the wages of sin is death; but the gift of God is eternal life through Jesus Christ our Lord."

I knew briefly the deeper theological interpretations of this particular verse: because of original sin death entered into the world. All humans must face death, but for the Christian, death is not the end of life but the beginning. Yet today, as I pondered this verse, I could not help but think of all the sins I had committed. Was it possible I was being punished? Was I going to collect my "wages" in the currency of death?

"All have sinned and come short of the glory of God." As if in answer to my unspoken thoughts this also familiar verse came to mind. *All* have sinned. *All* do not die from cancer. I am not being punished for my sins. My sins have been paid for already by One who suffered death in my place. To doubt that this was true was tantamount to blasphemy. If I did not believe Jesus came to "save me from my sins," to bear my iniquities, to offer unlimited forgiveness, and to give eternal life, then I did not have anything to live for. And absolutely nothing to die for.

Another kind of discomfort was also disturbing me this morning. I was self-conscious. Everyone in this building knew about my surgery. I didn't mind their knowing, but it did make me uncomfortable. The fact that my shape was not exactly the same on both sides (though it probably would have taken studied scrutiny to determine that) intensified my uneasiness.

It was almost the same feeling as knowing your underwear has a hole in it or your feet are dirty under your socks. You think, *What if I were in a wreck and everybody at the hospital saw it?* My thoughts were similar: *What if they could see my scar? my cotton-stuffed brassiere? the safety-pinned elastic connecting my panties to my bra on the left side to keep my "breast" from riding up?* Horrible thoughts! I longed for the day I could get my weighted, fluid-filled, natural-contoured prosthesis!

Thinking about my prosthesis reminded me of my new lump again. "If I have to have more surgery," I realized despairingly, "it'll be just that much longer before I can get it!"

Jim nudged me and I jumped, realizing belatedly that Brother Manning had asked the congregation to stand for the invitational hymn. I hurried to the piano. As I played, I thought about the words of the old, well-loved hymn that Jim was directing:

> Just as I am, without one plea,
> But that Thy blood was shed for me,
> And that Thou bidd'st me come to Thee,
> O Lamb of God, I come! I come!

Thinking of the words of Paul, I paraphrased: "I come to You, Lamb of God, troubled, yet not distressed; perplexed, but not in despair; persecuted, but not forsaken; cast down, but not destroyed. Just as I am, I come."

*　　*　　*

"I'm the Dairy Mart girl," Laura said, pad and pen in hand. "May I take your order?" Then, in a conspiratorial whisper, she added, "Everybody order banana splits—that's all I'm gonna fix!"

"I'd like a banana split, please, Miss," Jim ordered obediently.

"Me, too," echoed Pat.

"Make that three," I said.

"No, four," added Ross.

Carefully Laura wrote down the orders and put the paper in her apron pocket. In a surprisingly short time she returned with our banana splits, dripping chocolate syrup and topped with cherries.

"Mmm, delicious!" said Aunt Pat. "This doesn't have any calories, does it?"

"Thank you, Laura. This is really good," I said, appreciatively. She had learned to do so many things that were helpful to me and good training for her. She always made the popcorn; she could make excellent coffee; and she liked to surprise Jim and me with breakfast in bed on Saturdays. I encouraged her efforts in the kitchen; it gave her a feeling of pride and accomplishment to serve us and our guests.

Tonight I was making a concerted effort to be cheerful and to appear unworried. I was even staying up later than I knew I should. Pat had surprised us all by coming in a few hours ago so that she could be here for my surgery early Monday morning. This was my last evening at home before checking into the hospital.

The previous week had been a busy one. True to my resolve of last Sunday morning, I had told Jim about the lump. He was calm but concerned and suggested I see what Dr. Winslow had to say about it.

I had to wait almost an hour in his crowded reception room to hear the few words I knew in advance he was going to say: "That lump needs to come out."

"Yes. I know it does. But what does it feel like to you?"

"I'm not as sure about this one as I was the other, but all lumps need to be checked on and taken out. There is just no way to know for sure whether one is malignant or benign until you go in."

He sat down on the little stool in front of me, his yellow suit the only bright spot in the surroundings. He was always dressed smartly; today, however except for noticing the brilliant yellow, I was oblivious to the perfection of his attire.

When he sat down, I knew he had something else to say; I was sure it was important, or he would have remained standing and "thrown" it at me on his way out the door to see the next in a long line of waiting patients.

"I think you should consider having another mastectomy, even if this lump isn't malignant. If you are going to continue to have problems, and it appears that you are, the safest, least trouble-some thing to do is remove the breast."

He paused to let the full impact of his words sink in. Then, reading correctly the incredulous look on my face, he continued a little less bluntly:

"I know that sounds harsh; I just think you should consider it. That's what I'd recommend if it were my wife."

Knowing full well my own state of mind and physical condition,

I said exactly what I thought. "I don't think I'm ready for that yet. It's too soon after the first one."

He shrugged his shoulders. "Just think about it."

"I'll think about it," I said.

But I refused to think about it.

*　　*　　*

Dr. Kistler held up the blue-and-white "road map" of the inside of my right breast. I had already seen Dr. Garrett, who admitted that the lump *was* there, and he had sent me over to the hospital for a xerogram. Dr. Kistler had examined me also.

"I just can't say definitely about this one," he said. "I can *feel* the lump, but because of its position" (which was almost midchest and barely in the breast tissue itself) "we can't get a good picture of it."

I waited as he studied some more.

"I agree with Dr. Garrett that it's probably a fatty tumor; I also agree that if you are going to worry about it, we should schedule surgery and take it out."

"I don't want unnecessary surgery, Dr. Kistler, but I don't want to take any chances either. Nobody thought the last lump was cancer. It happened once; it can happen again."

Surgery was scheduled for Monday morning. Neither Dr. Garrett nor Dr. Kistler thought a simple mastectomy, as a precautionary measure, was called for at this time.

*　　*　　*

Now here it was, "hospital eve" again, and I was sitting on the couch eating a banana split as if tomorrow would never come. I thought back over the day, putting mental check marks by the things I had accomplished in the way of getting ready for another hospital stay: I had vacuumed the house, done the laundry, cleaned the bathrooms, washed Rick's and Lana's hair, put fresh sheets on all the beds, cleaned the oven, and baked chocolate chip cookies.

In addition, I had fixed three meals, gone shopping with Bernice while the kids were napping, fixed Mama's hair and cut Papa's, and entertained some unexpected visitors. When Pat came in after supper, we had talked awhile and then, at Jim's request, had worked on a song for her to sing in church tomorrow. That led to a "sing song"; all of us had gathered around the piano and had sung for at least an hour.

I was tired but happy. The day had been full and good. I wasn't too concerned about losing a few hours of sleep tonight; I could sleep tomorrow night when my family wouldn't be around trying so hard to keep my mind off my surgery!

*   *   *

Sunday, July 18, 1976

I'm writing this early Sunday morning before anyone else is up. I'm not going to take this journal with me to the hospital, so this will be my last entry till I return.

I've got to get everyone up soon to get ready for Sunday school and church. I'll go this morning, of course, but think I *might* miss tonight!

I feel like this is a replay of a previous episode in my life. It was just two months ago today, May 16, that I checked into the hospital for my mastectomy.

I'm not afraid to go—just eager to go on and get it over with.

I didn't get all the housecleaning done that I wanted to do but did get my kitchen all cleaned and my mending done!   I hate to leave Rick today. He always gets upset when *I* leave *him*. If *he* leaves *me*, he's okay! I may let him go home from church with Mama so he won't be here when I go.

The feeling of "replay" continued:

. . .the same talkative lady admitted me into the hospital; she commented, as she had the last time, that she knew my dad in college when I gave his name as "a relative not living at my address."

. . . again I was settled into a beautiful private room on Henderson; this time the jungle print was yellow.

. . . the nurses, surprised to see me again so soon, were the same ones who had made me so comfortable before; we enjoyed our little reunion although they were concerned about my surgery.

. . . the group gathered around my bed early Monday morning was almost identical to that of two months ago; again my Papa led a prayer for me and the doctors and nurses attending me.

. . . the same beautiful Recovery Room nurse came in and "hypnotized" me again; I was pleased that she remembered me when she commented, "I didn't expect to see you back up here!"

Coincidently, Dr. Garrett and I went up to surgery on the same elevator. I was surprised to find him there when my stretcher was wheeled through the doors.

"Glad you could make it," I commented dryly.

"Nothing better to do this morning," he retorted.

The elevator continued upward. The two stretcher attendants and a stiffstarched nurse were pretending not to hear this strange conversation.

Covered to the chin with a sheet and strapped to the stretcher, with my senses a little dulled by the hypo, I felt at a disadvantage for this kind of parley. Nevertheless, I got in one more shot: "Hope you're not as knife happy as you were two months ago."

"No, I'm a little tired this morning—been partying all night," he said straight-faced.

His smile answered mine, and I felt good about everything. I wanted to say, "I like you, Dr. Garrett. I'm glad you're going to be in there with me." But I didn't. That would've sounded corny.

I was transferred gently from stretcher to operating table, strapped again, with arms outstretched, and hooked up to numerous plastic tubes and other strange-looking apparatus. An O.R. nurse came over and pulled the sheet down to my waist. I caught her shocked expression.

"Two months ago," I replied to her unspoken question.

"How old are you, anyway?" she asked, reaching for my arm band to verify whatever I answered.

"Thirty-two."

Shaking her head, she stated flatly: "You're too young for that."

"Yeah, I told them, but nobody would listen."

I turned my head as Dr. Garrett came in, dressed in his leprechaun suit but still ungloved.

"I want to check one more time to be sure where it is," he explained as he palpated my breast. "I'd hate to cut out the wrong thing!"

"Just leave my legs alone," I quipped. Dr. Garrett knew what I was referring to. We had been discussing my adjustment to the mastectomy in his office a few weeks ago. I had shrugged my shoulders, as if to say, "It doesn't matter," and commented, "Jim's a 'leg man' anyway!"

However, even in my drugged state, I realized nobody else

would understand what I meant. *I'll bet that sounded funny*.

Two hours later I was back in my room "bright-eyed and bushy-tailed!" It was eleven o'clock (my surgery had been at nine), and I couldn't believe how good I felt. I was even hungry!

My whole "cheering section" had rejoiced with us over the good news—benign!—and gone home. All except Jim. He and I were talking and laughing, "high" on the wonderful report.

It seemed that everyone in the hospital came by to share the good news. The phone rang continuously and I took all the calls, sitting up in bed and feeling like a million dollars. With a little assistance from Jim, I even made it to the bathroom with no difficulty!

I explained to Jim that Dr. Garrett said it was just a small benign growth. He had removed it, stitched me up, and told me I could go home in a couple of days.

It had been almost 18 hours since I had eaten. I was really hungry. Glancing around the room for eavesdroppers, I whispered, "If they don't bring my lunch soon, let's sneak down the back stairs and go out to eat."

"I don't know, Momps," Jim replied. "I can't think of a place in town that will serve *unicorns*!"

"Jim—" I threatened, reaching for a magazine.

"Well," he reconsidered, "on second thought, in that hospital gown you could walk in backwards and maybe get by. There's *definitely* nothing missing *there*!"

I threw the magazine. And missed.

*　　*　　*

"Can I go home today?" I asked eagerly.

Dr. Garrett looked exasperated. "You just had surgery yesterday!"

"I know, but I feel *great*! There's nothing to this, compared to the last time."

"You're right about that; but still, you *have* had surgery," he explained patiently, "and you can't recover from that in one day. Ask me again tomorrow."

I wrinkled my nose in mock disgust. "I'll have my suitcase packed," I warned, "and I'm going to call Jim tonight and tell him to come get me tomorrow." I anticipated a challenge.

"All right, all right! You can go home tomorrow. But you'll have to come to the office in a week to get your stitches out. Other than that you can do pretty much what you want to do. Just don't use the right arm too much for a few days."

"Wait a minute!" I said as he headed for the door. "One more question!"

He turned, his expression suggesting he'd believe that when he heard it. I crossed my fingers and hoped as I asked the question that had been top priority in my mind for weeks: "When can I be fitted for my prosthesis?"

"Not until your mastectomy incision is fully healed and you can wear a brassiere comfortably."

"When?" I persisted. "How long do you think?"

He paused as if reluctant to answer. "At least another month."

Chapter Twelve

Time after time I have seen the damage that can be done to a woman if she belittles or hates herself after a mastectomy. The only way to achieve physical and mental well-being is to stand on your own two feet, and this takes the confidence that comes out of loving yourself and life. Remember these lines from Shakespeare, "Our doubts are traitors, and make us lose the good we oft might win, by fearing to attempt. . . ."

Reach to Recovery
Terese Lasser

The ideal life is in our blood and never will be still. Sad will be the day for any man when he becomes contented with the thoughts he is thinking and the deeds he is doing—where there is not forever beating at the doors of his soul some great desire to do something larger, which he knows that he was meant and made to do.

Phillips Brooks

What man is he that feareth the Lord?
him shall he teach in the way that he shall choose.

Psalm 25:32

The air was clear and still. Tall pine trees framed the calm, glassy surface of the cove water. Traffic, toy-like in the distance, crossed the bridge that spanned the water connecting Carrice Cove to Toledo Bend's expanse. The noise of the cars was drowned by the smooth humming of our boat engine, idling now as I struggled to manipulate the skis, the tow rope, and myself into position.

It was a perfect east Texas summer day—late August, sunny and hot. Its perfection was enhanced by the fact that ours was the only boat in our favorite skiing place, leaving us free to enjoy the water and each other with abandon. Today was the first time this summer that our family had been out in the boat together, a pastime we had thoroughly and frequently enjoyed for several years.

The boat wasn't fancy, but it was large enough to accommodate all of us easily, and deep enough to be safe for the two little ones. All I could see from my place at the end of the ski rope were the tops of Rick's and Lana's little heads and the shoulders of their orange-colored life preservers. Ross and Laura were more easily seen; their faces, even from this distance, showed concern. Jim, too, was looking my way, waiting for the nod that meant "tighten up and go!"

My teeth were chattering, but it was from nervousness — and a little fear — rather than cold. I wasn't quite sure I should be attempting to ski. Although I had Dr. Garrett's permission to do anything I felt like doing, it had been only five weeks since my last surgery and just three months since my radical mastectomy. The first incision was not yet completely healed and I was still weak.

I berated myself fiercely as I wrestled awkwardly with the skis. *You dummy! Nobody made you get out here. In fact, you'll remember your mother told you in no uncertain terms that you'd better not dare get on these skis. What if you pull something out of whack on that left side? What if you lose your balance and fall on your skis? You could hurt yourself badly. Obviously you don't have the sense of a goose.*

Defiantly the rebuttal came: *I have to do this. I have to prove to myself that I can still do anything I did 'before.' However foolish it is, I have to do it.*

My feet were securely positioned in the ski shoes, notch four. *At least you have sense enough to use two skis instead of the slalom*, I congratulated myself proudly. *That shows you're not totally crazy.* I knew it would be less strain on my arms and through my shoulders to come up on two skis rather than one. And although I was trying to prove something to myself, I didn't have to slalom today to do it. I knew if I could make it on doubles, I could eventually be skimming across the lake on my good old Alfredo Mendoza.

Tightening my grip on the handle, I shouted "Hit it!" The roar of the motor reached my ears a split second before I felt the surge of power. I held on, feeling the tremendous pull in my weakened arms. I wondered briefly if I should let go and wait till next summer, but before I had time to answer my own question I was up! *Joy! Look at me, world! I'm skiing!*

Following cautiously in the boat's wake, I took inventory: my arms were okay—a little weak but okay. Nothing was hurting. My legs were trembling from the unaccustomed strain, but that wasn't serious. With great care, I shifted my full grip to my left hand and lifted my right one to the heavens. "Thank You, Lord," I shouted into the wind-and-water spray rushing into my face. "Thank you for *everything*!"

I laughed aloud thinking of the care I had just taken to raise one hand, remembering the times I had put the ski handle between my legs and lifted both arms skyward in my "Cypress Gardens" pose. *There'll be time again for such bravado*, I thought happily. *Today, just skiing is enough.*

*   *   *

Floating lazily in the water, I watched Jim and the children playing and thought again how lucky I was to be alive! It wasn't until I had regained some of my strength and had begun to feel better that it dawned on me that I might have died. And might still! The reality of cancer was just beginning to hit me. I pushed the fears back into the far recesses of my mind; after all, I had been assured that all the cancer had been excised and my chances of living a normal life span were good.

"You'll outlive me," Dr. Garrett had promised heartily.

"That's not saying much," I replied. "You're an old man already!" He had just turned fifty, a fact he frequently alluded to. Actually, he appeared to be as fit as most men twenty years younger.

"Well," he revised his prediction reluctantly, "would you believe a hundred and one?"

With the sun on my face, the cool water lapping around me, and my family cavorting happily within my range of vision, the longevity he promised seemed very possible. There was no place for doubts and fears on a day like today.

Even my ridiculous swimming attire seemed more humorous than pathetic; the sunny side of everything today was so blindingly bright that it was impossible to see even a shadow of darkness. I glanced down at my bathing suit which had been a welcome hand-me-down from Janet. None of my two-piece suits was suitable, and I hadn't wanted to search seriously for a suit to meet my new requirements until I was healed and had my prosthesis. When Jan offered an old one of hers—one piece and not too low cut—I grabbed it eagerly. I had taken numerous tucks in the bodice of the black and white fabric and had stuffed the left side with a rubber pad from an old "push-up bra" and some pantyhose. The resulting outfit was merely passable; I wouldn't have worn it in public, but it was fine for a family outing.

Suddenly Jim popped up from the water right beside me, gesturing wildly. "Mamuk, the killer whale!" he gasped.

"Mamuk, the killer whale?" I queried frostily, eyebrows raised. (I was suspicious of an attack, but not from a whale!)

"I just saw it! Just below the surface—in fact, right about where you're floating! I saw this enormous black-and-white creature."

"Jim Nethery!" I screeched, as he gave my backside a pinch and disappeared beneath the water.

I swam warily around the boat and climbed up the ladder. "Mamuk may be a whale, but she's a lot like an elephant in one way—she never forgets!" I crawled out on the front of the boat and stretched out to get some sun. "You'd better not swim around this way," I threatened. "Have you ever had a whale hit you broadside from a dive off the bow of a boat?"

Sun bathing was something I had always enjoyed. The sun felt like a huge heating pad, covering my body and sending its delicious warmth throughout, even into my bones, relaxing, melting away tensions, soothing and restoring. As I relaxed, my thoughts skipped over the days since my last surgery, lingering fondly on some of the highlights. . . .

My brother, Raymond, had married a lovely girl, Karen, in a garden ceremony at her home. I had served at the reception, although it had only been a week since my surgery. I was uncomfortable and a little self-conscious—put together as I was with elastic, safety pins, and cotton stuffing! But their happiness and the beauty of the occasion overshadowed my discomfort.

The Weavers had spent a couple of days with us. We barbecued chickens and made ice cream, then stayed up half the night playing "You Don't Say" and "Password." It did me so much good to be with friends like them who knew me so well, had shared good times and bad, and made me forget that I was a "mastectomee." I had found already that some people were uncomfortable around me, some treated me as if I were contagious, and some tried to make me into an invalid. Larry and Nita just treated me like *me*.

My friend Joanna and her children had come for a day of swimming and picnicking at nearby Red Hill Lake. Both Joanna and Anita were expecting babies in November! I was a little envious. I had enjoyed being pregnant; it was painful to me to know that although we didn't plan to have more children, if we had, it would be too dangerous for me now. Knowing that both Anita and Joanna were going to nurse their babies, as I had Ross and Laura, made me even more wistful.

Jim and Lana had celebrated birthdays in August. Jim was

thirty-four on the ninth; Lana turned two on the twenty-fifth.

Overall, I reflected, *this past month has been a good one. And this wonderful day—the last 'play day' before school starts again on Monday—has been a perfect one to end a less-than-perfect summer.*

*   *   *

Despite Ross and Laura's protests, school began again. Soon we were settled into the routine of early rising, school buses, and lunch boxes. It was quiet on our hill with the two "big kids" gone, and it seemed strange not to be able to pick up the phone and call Bernice or Mama. I was really on my own now, and it felt good. *Too* good, probably, for I began to get overconfident about my abilities and strengths. I could not accept the fact that I was not back "up to par" and I continually tried to do (and *did!*) more than I should have. The results were fatigue and the beginnings of depression. As usual, I expressed my feelings in my journal:

September 6, 1976

It's 11 o'clock in the morning. I am frustrated and a little depressed. As well as I know with my *mind* that taking care of these kids and running this home smoothly is my most important task, I still yearn with my soul to paint, and sew, and write poetry, and *create*. But there's no time. I am efficient and organized. (No bragging, just fact!) Yet *still* there is no time to do all I want to do.

Right now I have several unfinished projects: an American Eagle hook rug; a beautiful wall embroidery (bicentennial) that I designed for Ross's room; two dozen egg shells blown, dried, and ready to be painted for Christmas ornaments; several pieces of material to be sewn; two poems that need to be polished; a bread-dough basket to be made; and a head full of Christmas ideas.

But *every* day there is washing, cleaning, and cooking to do over and over. And as good as Rick and Lana are, they require attention, at least indirectly, all day long. I am not happy if things aren't done around the house. (And a five-bedroom, three-bath house with four kids in it has a lot to be done to!)

Yet even when I feel frustrated, I know there's no place I'd rather be. If I could only be *satisfied* to be just a homemaker/mother for a few more years and not try to do all the extras that mean so much to me.

The most creative, rewarding thing I can do right now is mold these two babies into happy, healthy, well-adjusted little people during the few years they are home with me. I *know* that. *Why* do I keep beating my head against a wall trying to do more than any one woman can be expected to do? I'm *stupid*, that's why!

This morning I've made beds, fixed several breakfasts, showered and washed my hair, dressed Rick and Lana twice already (they played in their pool awhile outside), washed *their* hair, did three loads of laundry, cleaned the kitchen, "picked up" the house, refereed several squabbles, and read the paper. *Now* it's time to cook dinner!

I feel better already just writing all this down. Maybe it will help me get my priorities straightened out. I pray about it a lot. I know God gave us Rick and Lana just as He did Ross and Laura. He also gave me creative talents. Maybe for right now He wants my creative yearnings to be channeled in *their* direction. Not *maybe*. *I know* He does. Why am I pulled in so many directions? I guess I am one of God's difficult, self-willed children.

Rick still takes so much discipline. These are the important years, because they set the pattern for the years that follow. He must be trained to behave pleasantly and mannerly, to act in socially acceptable ways, to respond immediately to "commands," etc. I went through this type of training with Ross and Laura. And Lana's turn is beginning. I know how important it is not to let up in the training. It pays off. It makes for happy children (and happy parents) later. But it is so hard *now*. It would be so much easier to overlook or ignore bad behavior. Perhaps that is why some mothers give up and go to work! (And no wonder discipline is the number one problem in our schools today!)

At least, in spite of my groanings and moanings sometimes, I've never lost my "calling" to the job God gave me. I am a *homemaker*. And proud of it.

I put my pen down and reflected on what I had just written, determined to get to the root of the problem. I sorted through the various "negatives": frustration at being unable to do the "extras" that I enjoyed doing; the financial strain that kept us from pursuing favorite "outlets" such as movies, weekend vacations, going out for dinner; the responsibilities and confinement of two small children; my fears of recurring cancer; my largely unexpressed, but very real doubts about my attractiveness as a woman since my mastectomy; and my ever-present fatigue.

And sitting smack dab on top of the pyramid of problems that these things added up to was the one thing that made me feel the worst: *guilt*. I felt guilty about being frustrated; guilty about being dissatisfied; guilty about my fears; guilty about feeling guilty!

"Now we're getting somewhere," I thought triumphantly, as an unsuspected truth began to dawn. "I've been expecting *depression*; the devil sneaked up behind me with *guilt!*"

Help me, Lord! Help me sort this out. The devil is trying to make me feel guilty for being human. I can't let him do that! You *made* me human—that can't be wrong. It can't be wrong to have human feelings, either, can it?

Okay, what *is* "wrong" here? If it's not wrong to have human feelings, where does the guilt come from? It must be in dwelling on the negative feelings—nursing and cherishing them until they begin to take root and grow—that the guilt begins. At least I think that's true for me.

Instead of facing the facts as they are and admitting that there are very real problems that are causing my feelings, I've been kicking myself for being so weak and unchristian. The Pollyanna facade I've been wearing has been my attempt to present a positive, Christian front to everyone so that my witness to Your power to uplift, guide, and strengthen Your children would not be a disappointment to You.

I feel a great responsibility, Lord, to show others that You are all-sufficient in times of trouble. I truly believe You are; I have felt Your nearness and Your love. This is the greatest opportunity I've ever had to witness for You. I'm so afraid of blowing it.

I thank You for the sense of responsibility. I thank You that I can see a golden opportunity for service when one knocks me to the ground! I thank You for giving me the strength to present that optimistic front to those I meet from day to day.

Now, Lord, help me to get straightened out *behind* the front. I am admitting my weaknesses to You. Will You help me get them in the right perspective before they destroy my self-confidence, my effectiveness as a Christian, my pride in being a homemaker, and my job in living?

Will You take away the guilt, Father? Just leave me a realistic knowledge that the problems are there (I don't have to feel guilty about *that!*) and help me know how to deal with them constructively. Let me depend more on You.

Wait, God! Could that be the number one problem? Could it be that my stubbornness about not wanting to be dependent on anyone includes *You*? Oh, Lord, *that's* wrong. That's it, isn't it? I've been trying to make it on my own strength and I am so weak. I *hate* being weak, both physically and spiritually.

Hmm? I'm listening, Lord. Yes, I remember that verse. You said, "My strength is made perfect in weakness." Wait, let me look it up. . . . Yes, here it is. 2 Corinthians 12:9: "My grace is sufficient for thee: for my strength is made perfect in weakness."

And Paul answered: "Most gladly therefore will I rather glory in my infirmities, that the power of Christ may rest upon me. Therefore I take pleasure in infirmities, in reproaches, in necessities, in persecutions, in distresses for Christ's sake: *For when I am weak, then am I strong!*"

Thank You, Lord.

*　　*　　*

The very next day a totally unexpected crisis arose. My mother went to Dr. Winslow for her annual checkup, and he found a large mass in her abdomen. He referred her to a gynecologist in Lufkin.

I was worried; Mama had not been feeling well for months and had put off having her checkup. I recalled a conversation we shared last Sunday as I fixed her hair.

She seemed distracted, almost absentminded, as she handed me the rollers. "I guess I must be getting old," she finally commented. "I'm so tired I just can't *go* anymore."

It had been a busy, trying summer for her; she had every reason to be thoroughly tired. Yet there was more to it than that. She was weak; she wasn't sleeping well, and she was having pains through her chest. Still, she attributed the symptoms to the rough summer we'd all had. But I knew she was stubbornly putting off her checkup, an appointment she faithfully kept in early summer each year. I was beginning to suspect that something was wrong, and now I knew that she did, too.

"When are you going for your physical?" I asked for the hundredth time that summer. "You are being a little bit ridiculous, you know. How would you feel if I didn't take care of myself?

Here it is September; school has started again, and you still haven't gone. I can't understand that."

Then she said something that I was to remember very vividly later: "If there *is* something wrong, it'll be so far gone there won't be anything they can do about it."

I was shaken but persisted. "What if I'd said that?"

"It's different for you. You're so young—you have your life ahead of you."

I was becoming angry. "That's the silliest thing I've ever heard. And what's more, that doesn't sound like you at all. *Please* go get your checkup. For me?"

She had gone. And now we were both more worried than we had been before.

Her appointment with the doctor in Lufkin was less than a week later. But before even that brief time had elapsed still another problem arose. I found another lump in my breast.

I didn't mention it to anyone but Jim. I was beginning to feel absurd. The little story about the boy who cried "wolf" came to my mind. I couldn't bear to get everybody upset again over *nothing*; I was tempted to ignore the new lump. But what if it were cancer?

This just can't be happening! I thought despairingly. *Enough is enough.* I felt like a character in a soap opera with a poorly written script. The scenes were redundant and a little farfetched. Obviously I couldn't fire my Writer/Director; I had signed a lifetime contract. Besides, He was the only one who knew how the story would end. I did offer one small suggestion however. *Excuse me, Sir, but isn't it time to live happily ever after?*

* * *

Sitting in the tiny room where I was waiting to be fitted for my prosthesis, I recalled the advice given in the Reach to Recovery booklet:

> When fitting your permanent form, try to wear a dress, sweater, or knit that will really hug your chest—stripes are great, or wear anything that will give you a very clear look at the outline of your bosom through your clothes. Be sure that your form matches as closely as possible your other breast—from sides, bottom, front, and top. Make sure that the spaces from the front center of your body to each breast are equal, and that the nipples are on an even line.

I hadn't worn anything closefitting because my present makeshift shape wouldn't permit it, but I clutched a T-shirt in my hand. I was ready.

There was only one place in Lufkin that carried breast forms, and that was a medical discount pharmacy. I had been a little nervous about coming to such a busy, *public* place, but I was directed immediately and politely to the correct person, and no one seemed to think it was unusual that a young lady should be coming in to buy a breast!

The saleslady was courteous and helpful; the entire procedure took only about twenty minutes. The first step was fitting me with a brassiere on the part of me that was left to fit! This was simple enough and soon accomplished. The bra was lacy and feminine, but a little stiffer and more rigidlooking than the smooth-cuppd natural-contoured ones I had worn.

Step two was finding a prosthesis to fit inside the empty left cup that *exactly* matched my right breast. This took longer because I was not satisfied with a less-than-perfect match. It had to *feel* right and look right from every angle. The weight had to be the same. I had waited a long time for this, and I wanted to be completely satisfied with what I got.

I was disappointed that the line of breast forms carried here didn't include a form made specifically for radical mastectomies, with the little "wing" going up toward the shoulder. I could have waited and gone to a larger city and found one. However, I was impatient; I wanted to do business with a place easily accessible the future, and I could not afford a more expensive prosthesis now anyway. Besides, the fit of the one I found here was so good I was completely satisfied. I felt normal for the first time in three months.

Walking out of the fitting room proudly and with a light step, I went to the cashier (a man!) with no embarrassment and gladly paid the price. I was careful to get my receipt—the cost of breast forms and bras with pockets to hold them are tax deductible, along with drugs and medical expenses. The receipt, marked "surgical," was also necessary to file with my insurance company to cover the prosthesis.

Mama was waiting for me in a shop that adjoined the pharmacy. Next on our agenda for the day was her visit to Dr. Reid; also on the schedule was a visit to Dr. Garrett's office.

Chapter Thirteen

Familial aggregations of cancer have long attracted attention. Nearly everyone knows at least one person who has had several close relatives with cancer. However, cancer is a common disease and some such "clustering" of cases would be expected on the basis of chance alone. In studying this problem, the appropriate question is whether such clustering exceeds that to be expected on the basis of a random distribution of cases throughout the population and, if this is so, what is the magnitude of the excess risk among relatives of cancer patients?

Cancer Rates and Risks, Second Edition
U.S. Dept. of Health, Education, and Welfare

If we had paid no more attention to our plants than we have to our children, we would now be living in a jungle of weeds.

Luther Burbank

Truly the light is sweet, and a pleasant thing it is for the eyes to behold the sun:

But if a man live many years, and rejoice in them all; yet let him remember the days of darkness; for they shall be many.

Ecclesiastes 11:7,8

I walked slowly through the hospital corridors after leaving the radiation center. There was no need to hurry; Mama's surgery had just begun and would take several hours. I had been with Papa and the rest of the family in the tiny seventh-floor waiting room for about thirty minutes after Mama was taken from her room. We were all anxious and poor company; I had decided to go down to see Dr. Kistler about my new lump while we were waiting. It would only take a few minutes, and this seemed to be a good opportunity.

Dr. Kistler had concurred with what Dr. Garrett said the past Monday: "The lump is probably the same thing as the last one; let's wait a month and check it again." That was what I had wanted to hear. Now I put that problem in the back of my mind for the time being and focused all my thoughts and prayers on Mama again.

It was still hard to believe that my *mother* was in the hospital having surgery. Mothers just aren't supposed to get sick—at least mine never had been. I never knew a healthier woman. She had never been in the hospital except to give birth to her four children and the twin daughters she miscarried. She had always taken excellent care of herself; she loved her Lord, her family, and being alive. This couldn't be happening to *Mama!*

Don't be so pessimistic, I interrupted my thinking to caution. *Dr. Reid thinks it's just an ovarian cyst or benign tumor. He's just doing the hysterectomy because he thinks it would be best for a woman mother's age since he has to operate anyway.*

Nevertheless, I was worried. When I had seen her wheeled away on that stretcher I thought my heart would burst with love for her. How gladly, how *eagerly* I would have changed places with her. I had looked at the faces of her family, and I knew each one felt just as I did. The pain I saw through the tears in Papa's eyes was almost more than I could bear. He had been with her through so many years—loving her, cherishing her, protecting her. How helpless he must have felt knowing he could not go with her now.

When the elevator doors opened, I stepped quickly inside and pushed the button marked "7"—the surgical floor. My thoughts reached the destination before I did: I saw the room as it had been when I left it—full of family and friends keeping the wearying vigil for one they loved, lifting prayers heavenward, and sending love boldly through doors marked "No Admittance." The elevator stopped; the doors opened smoothly, and I stepped out.

The room was empty.

Unable to comprehend what I was seeing, I stood there dumbly. The elevator closed behind me, and I was totally alone. Suddenly, as if an afterthought, fear overwhelmed me. It began, sickeningly, in the pit of my stomach and crept steadily upward to my throat, threatening to choke me.

Something is terribly wrong, I realized as my mind began to function again. *What has happened? Where is my Mama?* I fumbled to push the elevator button. I still had no idea what to do; I only knew I had to get out of here. The dreadful, smothering feeling of "something gone wrong" filled the little room like a palpable mass.

Somehow I managed to get back to Henderson Wing. I walked slowly; my legs were weak from fear. I could see Bernice, Brother Larry, and others standing in the hall outside mother's room. As I drew nearer I could see the worry written on their faces. "Where is Daddy?" I asked softly, still not understanding the situation, but not wanting any of them to tell me. Someone motioned to Mama's room and I went in. Papa was there, standing by the window, and Jeannie and Stevie were sitting on the bed.

"Where is Mama?" I asked.

Papa answered: "She's in the recovery room." (*Thank God! She isn't dead. People don't "recover" from death.*) He did not continue, and I was forced to ask, "What happened?"

"They didn't do the hysterectomy; they removed the lump and sewed her back up."

"Papa, *tell* me. What did they find?"

His lips were quivering as he struggled to answer. "It was malignant."

"Malignant?" I asked stupidly, as if that were not a word in my vocabulary. Then, to verify what my mind wouldn't accept, I said, "*Cancer?*"

He nodded. Tears filled my eyes as I saw my daddy's face. I put my arms around him, wishing I could take away some of the pain. For a moment all my concern was for him. *O God! This seems so unfair. Not again! How can he take it again?* My thoughts were whirling. *How can a man stand it when three of the women he loves—his mother, his wife, and his daughter—are all stricken by the same terrible, incurable disease?*

I turned to my sister and brother. (Raymond was unable to

173

come till later.) We made futile attempts to comfort each other, and I tried vainly to get more information. Their answers were vague: "Dr. Reid just said it was malignant." "He said he'd talk to us later." "Mama'll be in recovery about an hour." (*What* was malignant? Did he get it all? What is her prognosis?)

I wanted to scream from frustration. I had to know something definite—I had to find out! Papa was almost helpless from shock; Stevie and Jeannie seemed to be expecting *me* to "do something." "And why not?" I thought ruefully. "I've been taking charge all their lives." It had seemed to come naturally, being the oldest child.

Suddenly I knew what to do. "I'll be right back," I assured them, and hurried out of the room. *The radiation center! They are my friends; they care; they'll help me. And they know Mama was having surgery this morning—we talked about her just a little while ago.* I realized that I was fast getting "in a state" myself and deliberately slowed my pace to a walk and my mind to a standstill. *I can't find out anything if I'm incoherent*, I decided sensibly.

But when I reached Dr. Kistler's office, all I could manage to stammer was "Mama. They just 'sewed her back up.' It was *cancer*." I know I must have looked frightened. I was. I must have appeared to be near emotional collapse. I was. *Whatever* image I projected, Dr. Kistler seemed to understand my feelings. He left the room after insisting that I sit down. "I'll find out for you," he promised.

His secretary, Patsy Bayer, took my arm and led me to a chair. Jean Dixon brought me some coffee. I was so grateful for them. I knew I was imposing on their friendship and good natures and interrupting their busy schedules; but they never even remotely implied that. They gave me exactly what I needed; concern, sympathy, and a place to "let go." The rage, frustration, and tears that I had controlled in front of Papa and the others was vented here.

When Dr. Kistler returned, he had the information he had promised. "It was lymphoma—cancer of the lymphatic system. I checked the chest X-rays she had made yesterday, and there seems to be evidence of involvement there, too. I'm sure Dr. Reid will order more tests to discover the extent of the cancer. Lymphoma is responsive to both radiation and chemotherapy; however, if there is widespread involvement, drugs are usually used alone."

We discussed other aspects of the situation, and when I left his office, I left feeling much better. (I can cope with "knowing"—it's "*not* knowing" that drives me up the wall.) I detoured by the sixth floor chapel before returning to Mama's room. There was Somebody else I needed to talk to.

*   *   *

Two weeks, I thought wearily. *Can it possibly have been only two weeks since Mama's surgery?* I sat down on the couch gratefully, still clutching the dustcloth that signified the last chore accomplished. Mama's house was spotless! And what a pleasure it had been for me to clean it thoroughly in anticipation of her return home. I had worked here almost all day yesterday and returned this morning to do a few "last minute" things such as put fresh sheets on the bed, do one last load of laundry, and dust the furniture.

The past couple of weeks had been exhausting for all of us. I had spent the first two nights at the hospital with Mama, doing for her what she had done for me several months ago. Papa had continued to teach his classes at school each day, but he made the trip to Lufkin and back each evening. Jim took up the slack with the kids and the house caused by my frequent absences to be with Mama. We were all ready for her to come home!

Six days after her first surgery she had undergone a second one—the incision had come open and had to be repaired. Other than that her recovery had been good, and she was scheduled to begin chemotherapy in Houston in about a month. Her attitude was good and her faith in God as strong as ever. The only thing that concerned me was that neither she nor Papa wanted to know the details—or even discuss her condition. I couldn't understand that, since my feelings were exactly opposite, but I had to respect their wishes. If this was their way of "coping," who was I to insist they face reality?

In thinking of the events of the past two weeks, I naturally thought of the day I had been to see both Dr. Garrett and Dr. Connell. The advice they had given was on my mind constantly: "A simple mastectomy, even if this new lump is benign, is the best route for you to take." Dr. Garrett told me to come back in two weeks; if there had been no change for the better he would put me in the hospital for surgery. Today was Wednesday; Monday was my "deadline," and the mass was even more pronounced than it had been.

I had told both doctors that it wasn't the loss of the breast that bothered me so much; in fact, I felt sure I would feel less "deformed" with *no* breasts than with one. My dread of another surgery was based on more complex considerations: leaving the kids again, burdening Jim with more worry and trouble, facing greater financial problems, being dependent on others again, going through a long recuperation period, etc. In addition to these factors, I felt like a traitor, leaving my mother when she needed me. And I hated to put her through the ordeal of my having major surgery when she was in such a weakened condition.

The present intruded loudly into my reverie in the form of children's strident voices. Rick and Lana were getting fussy. It was naptime, and I needed to get them home. I walked through the house one last time, checking to see that everything was in order. I sat down briefly on the edge of the king-sized bed in Mama and Papa's bedroom and lifted my thoughts to my heavenly Father: *Thank You, Lord, for my parents. I am so blessed to be their child. You have listened to my prayers of anguish and pain these past weeks; and I know You understood when I questioned "Why?" Today I come to You with thanksgiving in my heart; I still don't know the answer to "why" but I trust that You do.*

Thank You for Mama's beautiful faith that has been so evident and so inspiring. Thank You for the wonderful nurses who cared for her so well and so lovingly. Thank You for all the people who prayed for her recovery.

Please help me, Father. She will need me and I'm so tired. I am anxious about what the future holds for both of us. I am even fearful. Please give me strength to do what I have to do and let me not fail You in any way.

The kids and I went home; the rest of the day was as busy as the first. We visited with Mama a while after Ross and Laura came home from school; we went to Hemphill to watch Ross's junior high football game; and, of course, there was supper to fix and kids to bathe.

I wrote in my journal before going to bed:

I've been "teary-eyed" today—been crying a *lot* lately. The past few months have been the most stressful, most upsetting, of my life. And even now it's not over as we have mother's ordeal yet unfinished, I face more surgery, and Jim is not feeling well due to a prostate infection. Our financial situation is not good, either, yet we do have all we need. (And more than we need.)

But this is *life*. Troubles and trials are inevitable, and they can "make or break us." I pray almost daily not just for strength to endure, but for the wisdom to be drawn closer to God in all this—for eyes and heart open to learn the truths He wants me to know.

I need to grow so much more! I'm not yet fit for the kingdom of God, although something in me yearns to begin that great adventure to which death opens the door. It seems each day my eyes are opened to more areas in my self that need "realigning." (Or complete overhauling!)

I wrote several more paragraphs about the day's activities before closing, then glanced back over what I had written. *That "death" bit sounds almost morbid,"* I thought. *Would a psychiatrist call that a "suicidal tendency" or a "death wish"?* God knows I'm not ready to die, but He also knows I'm not afraid of it. *I think*, I continued, deciding to analyze myself, *that considering the events of the past few months, thoughts of death are normal. I think rather than wanting to die, what you are doing is facing the reality of death and knowing it would be heaven."* (Double meaning intended!)

Sunday, October 3, was my last day at home before leaving Monday to face whatever I had to face. I recorded the events of that day:

Jim got up early and went to Cat Holler with his dad to fix fence. The little kids and I got up about 7:30—the big ones at 8:00.

Went to Sunday school and church; I'm teaching Rick's class this new church year. He promoted from the nursery to the preschool class.

We ate dinner at Bernice's. Delicious!

After we got the babies down for naps, we had a slaughtering! Killed and dressed ten roosters. Bernice and Buddy, Stevie and Papa helped. We had them in the freezer in no time flat! (The *chickens!*)

Karen and Raymond came over. They want Ross and Laura to come stay with them next weekend.

Mrs. Speights and Mrs. Love brought some food today for Jim and the kids to eat while I'm gone. That was so thoughtful and sweet.

I took Rick and Lana to Hemphill to meet Jan. Both were glad to go which made me feel good. I don't know what I'd do without Jan. She *always* offers to help and means it. And I know the kids are happy there.

After church we went to Mama's to eat pancakes. Papa cooked them—his specialty! (And I cleaned up the kitchen.)

I was ready for bed at 10:00. I'm nervous about tomorrow. Isn't that silly?

*　　*　　*

"Breakfast is ready," I called from the foot of the stairs. I took the hot cookie sheet covered with cinnamon toast from the oven and mixed two large glasses of chocolate milk. This was Ross's and Laura's favorite breakfast. I fixed it today because it was probably the last breakfast I would fix for them for quite a while; I wanted it to be special!

I perched on the countertop with a cup of coffee and watched them fondly. Laura was fully dressed and ready for school; Ross, as usual, had barely managed to get his blue jeans on before I called! *They have to be the most beautiful, most wonderful children in the world,* I thought proudly. *And I'm not a bit prejudiced!* Laura's long, honey blond hair and green eyes were a contrast to Ross's dark hair and blue eyes; both were tall, healthy, and happy.

and happy. I enjoyed being around them and dreaded missing out on another week of their lives.

"Remember, I probably won't be here when you get home," I said reluctantly. "Laura, since Ross has football practice, you ride home on Dad's bus. I'm almost sure I'll have surgery in the morning; if I do, Daddy will come up tonight, and you will spend the night with Mama and go to school from there."

"Can't we go to the hospital for the surgery?" Laura asked. "It won't hurt if I miss one day of school."

"No ma'am. Not this time," I replied. "Remember how tired you both got when you went last May? Well, this surgery will be long, too. The best place for you is in school; besides, who would report to Mama what's going on in her room if you're not there?" Laura was in fifth grade, in a team teaching setup where my mother was head teacher. Of course Mama was out now, for an indefinite time, but she still liked to keep up and enjoyed hearing Laura's reports of activities there.

As they finished their breakfast, I packed lunch boxes. It was difficult knowing how to handle the problem of cancer with Ross and Laura. I tried to be honest with them and answer all their questions truthfully, but I didn't want to frighten them. I had reassured them (while trying to reassure myself) that the doctors said all the cancer was gone and this additional surgery was going to be just a precaution against my getting cancer in the other breast. I presumed I had succeeded in allaying any fears; I had my "antennae" out this morning and couldn't detect any uneasiness.

Both kids always kissed me good-bye before they left for school; they always said, "Love you," and I always said, "Have a good day." This morning Ross added, "I'll be praying for you." I watched from the front window until they were out of sight around the bend. They made a lovely picture: Ross was carrying Laura's big saxophone case, and she was carrying both lunch boxes and their books. They were laughing and lighthearted, and I was so glad. *Thank You, Father, for answering my prayer for them. Thank you for 'keeping their hearts in perfect peace.'* "

As I dressed, my thoughts were still on the children. Jim and I had worked hard at being good parents from the moment of their birth. Both of us took the responsibility of rearing them seriously. We had tried to provide love, security, and discipline in proper measure, and to see that disruptive, harmful influences were kept at a distance. But now, here was *cancer* — a disease that fostered fears and insecurities, often separated families by death, and, because of its well-earned reputation, was the most dreaded illness of mankind. This awful thing had intruded upon the lives of our kids not once but twice in less than six months. It was the most awesome challenge in our careers as parents.

This morning, as I reflected on the problem, an unusual perspective to the situation came to mind: *Rearing children is a lot like raising plants.* Picking up on the idea, sensing a comfort hidden in the thought, I worked out the analogy in my head.

Even before germination, a seed needs care. If the soil has been prepared ahead of time and is receptive, and if the elements (warmth, water, light) are suitable, the new plant has a much better start. Even so, the "seed" of a new human being has a great advantage when hearts are prepared and receptive for its birth, and when it is nurtured by love and good prenatal care.

After the seed has sprouted, proper care is essential to a healthy plant. It must have enough water, but not too much. Food and fertilizer are important, but a delicate balance must be maintained or the plant will suffer. Even so, a young child's formative years require an awesome amount of direction and care. Just as it's not enough to plant a seed and let nature take its course, it's never enough to give life to a person and then stand back and watch. Good nutrition is essential to attaining the maximum physical growth potential of a child. The eternal soul of each human being will soar upward to its destined height only through guidance, instruction, and example. A healthy, well-adjusted personality is formed by consistent love and discipline and by being fed regularly a diet of acceptance, appreciation, and self-worth.

Weeding around the plant is necessary so it is not choked out or bent so that it grows crooked or spindly. Occasionally, pruning is required to change the direction of growth or rid the plant of bruised or broken limbs that might stunt its growth. Even so, a "weeding" process is vital to the healthy development of a child. The world surrounding him is filled with undesirable influences that will take root quickly and threaten to choke proper growth. Wary parents must be constantly on the lookout for these "weeds" in the form of violent or immoral TV programs and advertising, bad habits acquired through example, or characteristics that are unattractive or detrimental. Curbing these harmful influences or attributes is a form of pruning; sometimes it is painful and tedious, but it is always worth the effort.

But there is one thing the gardener has no control over—the elements of nature. Storms, strong winds, dry spells, and heavy rains will come. The strong healthy plant, well-rooted and grounded (even sheltered to some extent), will be able to withstand the whims of nature. Even so, disasters are inevitable in the life of a human. No matter how much a parent wishes otherwise, illness, death, and accidents will happen. The strong, healthy child, well-rooted and grounded (even sheltered to some extent), will be *able to withstand the unavoidable storms of life.*

So, I continued my reflections, *if I make a practical application of this little mental exercise to the concern of my heart today—my children's well-being in the face of adversity—I will realize several things: First, I have done all I could to prepare them for this or any other unforeseen tragedy. Second, the problems of the past few months have been unavoidable; I must not fret over what I cannot help. Third, they are not standing alone, being buffeted and tossed about in this current "storm" of life. Their father and I are watching over them, guiding, directing, and sheltering them as much as we can.*

My heart was much lighter as I finished dressing and prepared to leave. *Thank You, Father, for directing my thoughts this morning. I feel better now about Ross and Laura. They're going to be just fine. You'll see to it, won't You, Father?*

I had insisted on driving myself to Lufkin. I felt fine, and there was no need for Jim to miss this day's work. I was looking forward to having the day to myself before my appointment with Dr. Garrett; I planned to visit Anita and Larry a little while, and Joanna was expecting me for lunch. I didn't mind a bit checking into the hospital alone; I had the procedure memorized by now!

Before leaving the house, I made a quick entry in my journal:

I'll just write a line before I leave for Lufkin. Don't know for sure if I'll stay today and check in the hospital or come back later. I am resigned now to the fact that I will have to have another mastectomy. I just wish we knew for sure it would be safe to wait a few months.

I don't want to go. I'm not worried or anxious—I just dread the ordeal.

I know God is with me. He is my comfort and my stay. And whatever else I lose, I can't lose Him!

Chapter Fourteen

It is now generally agreed that cancer of certain sites is associated with a very substantial excess risk of a second cancer in the same organ (skin, oral cavity, and large intestine and rectum) or in a paired organ (opposite breast, opposite ovary, perhaps opposite lung), presumably due to the same factors responsible for the first primary.

Cancer Rates and Risks, Second Edition
U.S. Dept. of Health, Education, and Welfare

I may die before morning.

What I must do is die now. I must accept the justice of death and the injustice of life. I have lived a good life—longer than many, better than most. . . . I have had thirty-two years. I couldn't ask for another day. What did I do to deserve birth? It was a gift. I am me—that is a miracle. I had no right to a single minute. Some are given a single hour. And yet I have had thirty-two years.

Few can choose when they will die. I choose to accept death now. As of this moment I give up my "right" to live.

High Prather
Notes to Myself

I am expecting the Lord to rescue me again,
so that once again I will see his goodness to me here
in the land of the living.

Psalm 17:13 LB

I climbed slowly up the back stairs that led directly to Henderson Wing, carrying my suitcase, my purse, and some books and magazines. I had parked the car almost at the foot of the entrance; I didn't intend to be anywhere but on Henderson, and bringing my things on up this way would save steps. I had not yet "checked in" but Dr. Garrett had called from his office and told Admissions I was coming.

Cheerful greetings were mixed with looks of surprise as the nurses saw me and my suitcase. Several of them gathered around the nurses' station, curious and friendly; they asked about me and about Mama, and it was like "old home week" for a few minutes. Then I explained about my surgery in the morning and asked about the availability of a private room.

I noticed some crestfallen looks and hastened to add: "Even a broom closet will do—I just want to be here with all of you. You seem like family since I spent so many days here after my surgeries and Mama's."

"We don't have any private rooms empty," someone said reluctantly, "and semiprivate doesn't look any better." (When Mama had checked in she had gone to a semiprivate room until a private one was available.) "Wait a minute," said Mrs. Waller, and we all turned expectantly to her. "Almost all our OB rooms are empty. We can put you there for now and move you if we get a run on babies. Just tell them at the desk that 212 is ready for you."

I hesitated. "Is this going to get anyone in trouble?" They assured me that it wasn't. "The room is empty, and it's no different from the other private rooms except that it's closer to the babies. Besides, you're *our* patient and you belong *here*!"

Soon I was settled in, grateful to be here with people I knew in a place that felt almost like home. It was five o'clock before I got my telephone; I called Jim immediately. Laura answered and called her daddy in from the basketball court where he was playing with Ross.

"Hey," he answered, a note of relief evident in his voice. "I was getting a little worried. Are you at the hospital?"

"No, I'm in the bridal suite of the Holiday Inn," I answered mischievously.

He laughed. "I'll be right there. Call room service and order dinner for two!"

"Can I take a rain check? I lied. I'm in 212, Memorial Hospital. And they've already served dinner. What are your plans for tomorrow morning?"

Serious now, he asked, "What time is your surgery?" I explained that it was scheduled for midmorning and suggested that he just wait and come tomorrow. "Are you sure you're okay? I can come on up and spend the night at Ken's."

"I'm just *fine*," I insisted. "I'll need you more tomorrow night. You'll sleep a lot better there and have plenty of time to get here in the morning."

"Will you call if you need me?"

"You know I will. And Jim, call the folks and tell them when surgery is. Talk to Mama and tell her I'm fine and sounded cheerful and wasn't a bit worried! Okay?"

"Okay. Sleep good. I love you."

"I love you, too. Good-bye," I held the phone for a few minutes, not wanting to completely break the connection between us. I *was* fine. I truly *didn't* need him to come up tonight. *Yeah, and those aren't tears running down your cheeks either, are they?* I asked myself derisively as I brushed them away with the back of my hand.

Putting the receiver down slowly, I continued unpacking my suitcase, again placing my Bible at bedside. Laura had made another "hospital book," and I sat down on the bed to look at it again. She had included some delightful thoughts:

Dear Mom,

I wish you didn't have to go, but you need a rest and I hope you get a good one. We'll miss you ever so much and we'll hope and pray that they get it all.

Love,
Laura (better known as "Leaky!")

I wish I was a magician,
As magician as one could be.
I'd make my *Mom* and *Grandma*
Not have surgery!
Author Unknown
(Very Unknown!)

When you go to the hospital
I will not be so gay,
But when you get home from the hospital
I hope you will be home to stay!

Following the poems were family pictures and space for visitors' signatures. Like the first book four months ago, it was something I would always treasure.

Jeannie was my first visitor; she came by after she got off work. Her questions were mostly about mother. I assured her that she was doing fine and was well taken care of—her sister Io was spending a few days with her.

"Has she wanted to know anything yet?" she asked.

"No! You'd think all she had was an ingrown toenail!" This was something all of us children were perplexed about. Our parents had always been so down-to-earth and realistic; we could not understand their pretense and evasiveness now. Spurred on by their failure to do so, I searched constantly for information about lymphoma. I felt that *someone* in the family had to "know" and by solitary vote (mine!) I was elected. I realized that of my own volition I was picking up the burden of knowledge that they didn't want to carry. Now I felt like "big sister" not only to my siblings but also to my parents.

I had called the toll-free Cancer Hotline number for our area, and they had sent me valuable booklets and information and answered all my questions. (I told Mama and Papa I had called; neither asked what I found out.) I talked to Dr. Garrett, Dr. Connell (who had checked on Mama regularly while she was in the hospital although she was not her patient), and Dr. Winslow. My parents knew all this. I even suggested that Papa talk to Dr. Winslow, since they both put so much faith in him. He didn't; nor did he ask me what any of them said.

I changed the subject. "By the way," I said in my most authoritative big-sister voice. "Have you gone for a physical and breast check yet?" Receiving a negative shake for an answer, I continued, "You'd better do that. I'm sorry about it, but my having breast cancer has put you in a high risk group, the risk is twice as high if you have a mother or sister with breast cancer." I was not trying to frighten her; I just wanted her to realize the risk and to start having regular breast checks.

We talked for a while about other common interests—our children, Diboll church activities and mutual friends, and what our brothers were up to; then she left to go home and fix supper. "I'll be back in the morning," she promised and kissed me good-bye.

After she had gone, I continued to think about the role cancer had played in our family. My daddy's mother had died from cancer of the female organs, my mother had lymphoma, and I had breast cancer. "What does all this mean to my daughter?" I wondered, heartsick. "Her mother, her grandmother, and her great-grandmother have had cancer. I wonder what *her* risks are? I knew that *my* having breast cancer placed Laura in a higher risk group; having two other blood relations with known cancer surely made it even higher. Yet Dr. Kistler had assured me that mother's cancer and mine were not related and had no connection whatsoever. But I wondered. . . .

*   *   *

I couldn't get to sleep. The "pill nurse" had given me a prescribed sleeping tablet an hour ago; everything was dark and quiet except for the usual hospital noises, and I wasn't hurting anywhere or uncomfortable. There was just a nagging, worrisome fear building up inside me that I couldn't seem to put my finger on. After tossing and turning for hours, I finally identified it: I was afraid I was going to die tomorrow.

The revelation was horrifying. No wonder I couldn't sleep—

my subconscious was entertaining an uninvited and very unwelcome guest: Death! I lay quietly trying to understand why I felt so fearful. Is it intuition? I know I am sensitive to "undercurrents" most people don't notice (not ESP; just a strong *awareness* of things and thoughts), but could I possibly have a premonition of my own death? I dismissed that as quickly as possible and moved ahead; there must be some concrete *realities* upon which my feelings are based.

Slowly I sorted it all out and came up with some fragments of thoughts which, when pieced together, must have caused my "computer" to come up with *death* as the outcome.

I remembered the tremendous amount of blood I had lost when I had the first mastectomy; would this happen again tomorrow?

I thought of a good friend of mine, a dedicated Christian mother my age, who had had a hysterectomy while I was still taking my cobalt treatments. For no apparent or expected reason, she had "died" on the operating table. Fortunately, she was revived after several minutes with emergency resuscitation measures, but I remembered it vividly. Couldn't this happen to me, too?

I also realized what a staggering load I was asking my body to carry by having so many surgeries in so short a time. In less than four months I would have had (if I lived past tomorrow) two lengthy, major surgeries, one minor one, and 25 cobalt treatments; that's asking a lot of a human body, isn't it? I knew how very tired and weak I was right now. Could I endure another surgery?

Finally, there was the fear that had been with me since childhood that I was going to die with cancer.

Wow! I thought, amazed. *I hadn't realized I'd been thinking about all that. No wonder I've secretly approached this surgery with an inexplicable dread!* Now, obviously, the next step was to ascertain whether or not my fears were valid. After brief contemplation, I realized to my dismay that I could not dismiss any of the points in question as being completely foolish. I *could* bleed to death; my heart *could* stop beating on the operating table; my body *could* be too weak to withstand the rigors of surgery; tomorrow *could* be the realization of my cancer-death fear.

Along with the startling realization that these were all real (though remote) possibilities came the peace I had been searching for. Now that the hidden fears had been brought out into the open, they were not so frightening. There was not one thing imagined that God could not take care of; and, if He chose *not* to, there was not one thing imagined that could separate me from His love!

Oh, God, let me put these fears in Your hands and be done with them. I would have done it before now, but I didn't know they were there! Isn't it funny—it was not death that was frightening me, it was the fear of death that frightened me! You know, Father, I would welcome death tomorrow if I knew that were Your will for me. But Father, if it is possible, please let me have the gift of life for a while longer. My family still needs me so much.

You entrusted Jim and me with four precious souls. Surely I haven't accomplished all that You want me to do for them. Ross and Laura both have a strong faith in You already, but they still need guidance. Rick and Lana are so young, Father! I've barely begun leading them to You.

I've always felt that my greatest contribution to the world and You would be through the lives of my children. Yet lately I've thought so often about the verse of scripture that you "gave" me back in 1968: "Ye have not chosen me, but I have chosen you, that you should go and bring forth fruit, and that your fruit should remain: that whatsoever ye shall ask of the Father in my name, he may give it you" (John 15:16).

I remember how important that verse became to me; I saw it everywhere I went and heard several sermons preached on it during a short period of time. I still think of that verse as "mine," and although I have chosen to ignore it and You often since then, I've never lost the conviction that You have chosen me to do something. . . . I'm not sure what it is, Lord, but how can I do it if I'm dead?

There's nothing else to say but this, Father. I put my life, along with those silly fears, into Your hands. Whatever You decide will be just fine with me.

I closed my eyes and slept.

*   *   *

The bath water was hot and deep; I lay back, determined to stay in the water as long as possible and savor every moment. This time I knew for sure it would be my last full bath for quite some time. There was time to relax for a while since my surgery was scheduled for later, and I knew none of the family would be here this early.

The fears of the previous night had dissolved into a faint apprehension; if someone had asked me to state my feelings in concrete terms I would have said: "I think I'm going to die, but I'm not afraid." I was up to my chin in bath water, but God's love surrounding me was even closer and warmer and more real. I hadn't had any pre-surgery medication yet, but I felt slightly detached from reality and almost euphoric. I had reached that "state of bliss" that one enters when he knows that everything is out of his hands, to worry is totally useless and time-consuming, and "what will be, will be."

I took the tiny bar of soap from its wrapper and began to wash my body. Gently—*very* gently—I passed the washcloth over my left side and arm. The sensation of numbness was still so strong and unpleasant that washing and shaving on that side was almost unbearable. I lathered the other side, and as the cloth passed over my right breast, tears sprang into my eyes. "In a few hours you won't even *be* there," I said sorrowfully, not even thinking how ridiculous it was to be talking to a *breast*. The tears fell onto my breast, making little paths through the soap lather that covered it. *This is dumb*, I thought, and reached for the towel to dry my eyes. *It's only a breast, after all.*

Only a breast. Just another part of the body. No different from losing an arm or a kidney or your tonsils. But I could not convince myself of such an obvious untruth. This breast was *not* just a part of my body; it was part of my *femininity*. It did not *make* me feminine, true, but it was a *symbol* of it. I remembered the thrill of that first brassiere, purchased more for my budding vanity than for the infuriatingly slow-blossoming (to my hurry-up mind, at least) breasts. I remembered learning as a teen-ager how fascinated boys were by the female breast; later I gained a fuller knowledge of what a vital role the breast plays in men's ideas of a woman's physical attractiveness. I remembered the joy of sharing myself and my body with Jim; I had been thankful for a slender, pleasant body and shapely breasts to give to the man I loved. I remembered the unspeakable thrill of holding my firstborn to my breast and watching him nuzzle instinctively for the nipple and "latch on," contentedly finding the nourishment for his little life from my body. Amazing! Delightful! So satisfying for us both.

Now I sat here, in a hospital bathtub, tearfully eulogizing the imminent death of my breast as if it were an old friend. And, in truth, it was.

*   *   *

I had just donned the unflattering hospital gown and crawled back into bed when a nurse entered. "I've got a shot for you, honey," she said. "They'll be coming for you in just a little while."

"What?" I screeched, my jaw dropping a foot. "They can't! My surgery's not till later! There was somebody else scheduled before me."

"Yes," she replied calmly. "That one didn't take as long as expected." *(Did he die on the operating table? Was it "open and shut" like Mama's?)*

I'm not superstitious, but things were off to a bad start. I hiked my gowntail up resignedly; you don't argue with a needle-wielding nurse. But my thoughts were whirling: *Jim probably hasn't even left home yet! Nobody will be here to tell me good-bye! I may not ever see any of them again.* When the nurse had gone, I reached for the bedside phone and made a long distance call home. No one answered; hope soared! At least he was on his way!

The injection was beginning to take effect. I had time for one more call.

"Hello . . this is Anita."

"Anita, has Larry left the house yet?" I knew he was planning to be here for my surgery and could probably come on at this inconvenient time easier than Jeannie or Linda, my two other choices.

"No, he's eating breakfast. Is something wrong?" she asked anxiously.

"My surgery's been rescheduled—they're coming to get me in a few minutes. Nobody is here; Jim's on his way, but I'm afraid he won't make it. I need somebody to *be* here. Can Larry come on now?" She assured me that he could come immediately. I replaced the phone feeling a little calmer. All I could do now was wait.

Five minutes later the door opened and Jim walked in! I was never so glad to see anyone in my life. "What are you *doing* here?" I asked inanely, my arms around his neck.

"I couldn't sleep, so I just decided to come on early." He paused, looking closely at my face. "Is something wrong?"

I explained the situation as well as I could in my sedated condition; we were holding hands through the raised "crib" rails when Brother Larry came in a few minutes later. Following closely on his arrival came the rest of my family—Papa, of course, and Bernice, and my sweet Aunt Io who was "substituting" for Mama. I could hardly believe they had all arrived before surgery! *Thank you, Father! You have to stay "on the ball" to keep ahead of upset hospital schedules, don't You?*

Aunt Io brought me my mother's love and the assurance of her prayers. She held my right hand, and Jim relinquished my left one to Papa for a few minutes. I was so overwhelmed by the love surrounding me that tears filled my eyes. I closed them quickly so no one would notice and get upset. I asked Papa to get my Bible and hand it to Bernice. "Please read the twenty-third Psalm for me—I didn't have time to read it before the nurse came in."

Her beautiful voice read the familiar, comforting words that had reassured me before my previous surgeries. "Yea, though I walk through the valley of the shadow of death, I will fear no evil: for thou art with me. . . ."

The door opened again. It was time to go.

Chapter Fifteen

Based on known doubling times of breast cancer cells, we are now certain that in almost every instance of the discovery of a breast tumor, there was a pre-clinical duration of that patient's disease for three to five or more years. We can calculate that there are at least 245,000 American women walking around today with a breast cancer at some stage of growth. And we know that survival is directly related to the stage at which the tumor is found and treated.

ACS President Benjamin F. Byrd, Jr., M.D.
Cancer News, Summer 1976
American Cancer Society

I am not tired of life, but when the Lord calls me home I shall go with the gladness of a boy bounding away from school.

Adoniram Judson

Though he slay me, yet will I trust in him.

Job 13:15

A sea of faces swam around me whenever I tried to open my eyes. They looked vaguely familiar, but I couldn't quite place them. I closed my eyes tightly, trying desperately to get back down into the deep, dark nothingness where the hurting couldn't reach me. It was impossible; people were touching me, talking to me, insisting that I respond to their attentions.

The faces *were* familiar! That's Jim . . . and Papa. . . . Other faces appeared above me—Bernice, Aunt Io, Jeannie, Linda, Brother Manning, nurses and *more* nurses. *I must be back in my room! I didn't die! But what happened? Why didn't I wake up in the recovery room like I always did? Surely I had regained consciousness there or they wouldn't have let me out!* I struggled to remember. . . .

Yes, I remembered something: I had been freezing cold and my teeth were chattering wildly. I heard Dr. Garrett say my name, and I had really *tried* to listen, but I could barely see him and his words didn't register. I think he said everything was all right. Wouldn't I remember if he'd said "cancer?"

My head was throbbing wildly; I was more conscious of pain there than in my chest. I decided to try my voice. "My head hurts. Can I have a shot?" A nurse answered, "Let's wait just a little while, honey." Ice water was brought and cold washcloths were kept on my forehead. (*Where is my mother? She's supposed to do that.*)

Blankets were piled on my bed in what seemed a vain effort to warm me. Nurses constantly checked the I.V. flow, my blood pressure, my pulse. No one would give me a drink of water, but somebody always held the little pan to my face when I vomited. No one would make the pain stop, but somebody was always there to share it. Eventually the nurses brought injections for both pain and nausea. Both were ineffective.

I drifted in and out of consciousness, seemingly unable to wake up. Hours passed—hours of pain and nausea and cold. The smiles and cheerfulness of those around me had long since turned to concern and anxiety. I knew they were worried. I was not snapping out of it. I wasn't acting like *me*. I wasn't "acting" at all—I couldn't even *pretend* I was okay at this time. I felt so bad—so totally *beaten* —that I would have preferred death. No thoughts of thanksgiving at being alive filled my heart; no sympathy for my bedside "mourners" stirred me to smile for their sakes; remembering the children was not sufficient stimulus to arouse my desire to live.

I heard Dr. Garrett's voice and opened my eyes to see him leaning over the bed. "Do you remember what I told you in the recovery room?" he said softly. I shook my head; I *didn't* remember. I didn't even care. "Everything is all right," he continued. "There was no malignancy. I did a simple mastectomy. You are going to be just fine." He spoke in simple sentences, as if trying to convince a child that his skinned knee was not fatal.

I merely nodded that I understood. It was easier than saying what I really thought. I wanted to scream to everyone in earshot: "Everything is not all right! *I'm* not all right. My *body's* not all right—it doesn't want to live. It's heavy, and it's dragging me down. I'm so tired. Leave me alone. Let me go with it." I wanted nothing in the world so much as to go to sleep and not wake up.

But Jim insisted on holding my hand in his so that I couldn't leave. The others went home, after being assured by the doctor that I was okay, but Jim stayed at my side. All night long he sat up, wiping my face with a cool cloth, holding the pan and calling the nurses when I vomited, feeding me tiny pieces of ice. He was my lifeline, *willing* me to respond to the medication, insisting that I make an effort to live, forcing me to smile at his corny, wee-hours wisecracks. ("How do you expect me to sleep with you throwing up every five minutes?" and "You think *you've* got troubles! I can't find my pet unicorn!")

The interminable night finally passed; Jim and I, both exhausted, greeted the dawn with hope, thinking *surely* I would begin feeling better soon. I didn't. Breakfast came, but just the sight of the tray made me sick again. With Jim's assistance I could make it to the bathroom; but each time I stood up, the already pounding headache crescendoed unbearably. When I got back in bed I was shaking uncontrollably and freezing cold again.

Jim had planned to stay until his mother could get here to spend the day; but when Aunt Imogene arrived (another of Mama's sisters) and graciously offered to stay with me, he accepted gratefully and left me in her capable, loving hands. I kissed him good-bye and gave him emphatic instructions to tell Mama I was feeling fine and not to worry. I wanted him to go home; there was really nothing else he could do to help me, and if he stayed longer Mama and the kids would start to worry.

When Bernice arrived, she was shocked to find me *still* so sick and lethargic. She immediately went to the nurses' station and requested that a "No Visitors" sign be put on the door. I was glad; I didn't want to see *anyone*. The day passed in much the same manner as the previous night; the pain and nausea, interspersed with chills and accompanied with a constant fever, continued; and the ineffectual injections were given regularly. I could not eat or sleep or find any comfort.

I was in the bathroom late that afternoon when someone knocked on my room door. Bernice left me momentarily, perched precariously and clinging to the convenient handrail, and admitted Dr. Garrett. "You can't come in," I joked weakly, as I stumbled toward the bed, clutching my "pancake" and Bernice's arm. "You're the man who did this to me!"

"I'm sorry," he said. "Still feeling pretty bad?"

I gave a brief recitation of my troubles, ending with the fact that I hadn't been able to eat a thing since surgery. "Just think how slim and sexy you'll be," he replied facetiously. I groaned. That was absolutely the last thing on my mind at the moment.

Carefully he untied the hospital gown and slipped it down over my right shoulder. Checking the bandages, he assured me that everything looked fine. "Then why am I so sick? Why do I have a fever? Why won't my head stop hurting? Did I have to have a blood transfusion this time?" I bombarded him with questions.

"It's only the day after surgery!" he answered patiently. "Give yourself *time*. You were weaker to start with, you know. I'm sure the headache is just tension. And no, although you lost a lot of blood, we managed to avoid a transfusion. I promise you'll feel better tomorrow."

I accepted his verdict meekly; I felt like there was more to it than that, but I *wanted* him to be right. His next words, however, gave me further cause for anxiety.

"I've got to go to a medical convention in Chicago. I won't see you again before you leave." Seeing my look of dismay, he held up his hand. "Now wait a minute! Dr. Connell will be checking on you, and Dr. Gonzalez is taking my hospital rounds. He'll take good care of you and dismiss you when you're ready."

"You can't *do* that!" I objected. "It's against all professional ethics to go off and leave a dying patient." He laughed. "It's not funny," I said firmly. But I smiled and wished him a good trip. His leaving made me feel even worse; I had taken it for granted that he would be there to take care of me.

*　*　*

I'll bet I look like death warmed over, I thought half-heartedly, not really caring at all. *I know that's what I feel like.* I was lying perfectly still, trying not to stir up the pain that was a little easier when I wasn't moving. My eyes were closed, but I knew Bernice was sitting quietly in the chair beside me. It was early evening; my condition had not changed.

"Bernice?" I whispered. "I've got to go to the bathroom." I had put it off as long as possible because of the pain involved with moving. I sat up as slowly as I could, but still the blinding pain struck my head like a sledgehammer. A few minutes later I was back in bed, shaking all over, freezing cold, and in awful pain. At that moment the door opened and in walked Papa and Laura!

Oh, no! I thought despairingly. *I don't want Laura to see me like this.* I stiffened my body and gritted my teeth to stop the shaking, but there was nothing I could do about the wave of nausea that was coming. "The pan—" I gasped and barely managed to wait till Bernice hastily put it under my chin. "I'm sorry," I apologized. "That was some way to greet two of my favorite people."

A few minutes later Papa and Laura "dismissed" Bernice so that she could get home before too late. Jeannie planned to spend the night with me, and Papa and Laura said they'd stay until she came. I hoped fervently that I wouldn't throw up again until Jeannie arrived; Papa had cared for all of us through childhood illnesses as often as Mama, but whenever the vomiting started, he either left the room or joined us!

Things went smoothly for a while. Laura had gone to the cafeteria for a cheeseburger and was eating quietly in the corner of my room. Papa was reading a magazine. Then I felt the sweat break out in a film covering my body and the nausea start building in the pit of my stomach. *Oh, no! I can't be going to vomit again*, I thought weakly. *Where is it all coming from?*

"Papa, I'm sorry but—" I grabbed my mouth, and he grabbed the pan. Just in time! I filled the pan and more; it overflowed onto my bed and gown. Stoically, Papa stood there until I had finished. Then he rang for a nurse, emptied the pan in the bathroom, and came back to my side as if nothing unusual had happened! I had always known there was nothing in the world my daddy wouldn't do for me—except, maybe, what he'd just done! Now there were no exceptions!

Papa stepped out of the room while the nurses helped me into a fresh hospital gown; then, he came back and stood beside me while they changed the sheets. Laura, with a sudden loss of appetite, had thrown away the remainder of her cheeseburger and was sitting curled up in a corner, concerned but helpless. I sat on the chair closest to the bed, blanket covered and shivering. The nurses finished their chores and left; still I sat, not ready to risk moving again just yet. As if on cue, Dr. Connell walked in, stage right, and found us motionless, ready for the next act (Or the *final curtain*, depending on the Director!).

I came alive! Here was someone who could help me! "I'm so glad to see you," I exclaimed. "You've got to *do* something—I can't stand this much longer!" She listened closely to everything I said, interjecting pertinent questions. When I had finished she made a suggestion: "Let's change your medication; it sounds like you are having a bad reaction to the pain shot—or maybe to the anesthetic you had. You really *should* be feeling better by now. I can't explain the fever; there must be a slight infection somewhere. I just don't know; but maybe changing the medication will help."

Shortly after she had gone, a nurse arrived with a shot; within minutes I was resting comfortably for the first time since surgery!

*　　*　　*

Jeannie was a good "nurse" and, because I was resting a little easier, we didn't have a great deal of difficulty through the night. However, she didn't get much sleep and was dreading the long work day ahead. She hadn't been gone long when Aunt Imogene came again to check on me and to see Mama, who was coming to Lufkin this morning to get her stitches out. I was eager to see Mama, too, and made an effort to get "prettied up" a little. Putting on a gown of my own and combing my hair helped my appearance considerably. But I still *felt* lousy.

The medication change had helped, but my head was still hurting, and the nausea refused to go away. My temperature continued to run above 100 for no apparent reason. Dr. Connell made her rounds early and was disappointed to find me not much improved. She ordered a blood test and a urinalysis and promised to check on me again later. "Has Dr. Gonzalez been in yet?" she asked. I replied that he hadn't. "You'll like him," she promised. (Here we go again!)"He's an excellent surgeon; all his patients are crazy about him because he is so understanding and really takes care of them. And that's not all," she added cryptically.

"Oh?" I asked, intrigued.

"You'll see," she replied, and she vanished out the door.

It was late morning when Mama came; Aunt B., her brother's wife, and Aunt Biddie, another sister, were with her. I was glad to see them all, but *especially* my mother. She looked so good; no one would have believed she was here having surgery just two weeks ago. Our concern for each other soon bordered on the ludicrous: I kept telling her to sit down, and she kept telling me to lie still and be quiet!

When the others got ready to leave, Mama announced that she was staying. "Staying?" I asked, astonished. "What do you mean *staying*? Is something wrong? Did Dr. Reid send you back to the hospital?" I was suddenly frightened that she was having difficulties no one had told me about.

"No, silly! I'm fine. I'm just going to stay here where I belong and take care of you," she explained.

"You can't do that," I said, hoping desperately that she *could*. "You need to be in bed yourself."

"Well then, I'll *go* to bed—right here on this cot," she said, plopping down on it to illustrate. "I'll rest better here where I can keep an eye on you. And what safer place for me to be than in a hospital?"

I didn't argue. I was delighted.

* * *

When my dinner arrived, Mama took over. "Doesn't that look

good!" she exclaimed about something. "*I know* you're going to like *this*!" she said, uncovering something else. I tried. I truly did. She stuck a straw in that little bowl of lukewarm soup and I sipped dutifully, ignoring the ominous rumblings from my stomach. It was no use. "I can't. It's all going to come back up if I take another sip. *You* eat it." Resigned to the fact that I wouldn't, she did.

Most of the day was spent resting quietly, protected by the "No Visitors" sign; occasionally one of the nurses would come in to say hello to Mama or to check my vital signs. As if I didn't have enough problems, my Hemo-Vac developed a malady of its own. (An air leak, I presumed, since it quit "suctioning.") Dr. Gonzalez was notified when the nurses gave up on fixing it.

"You'll see," Dr. Connell had said, and I "saw" when Dr. Gonzalez arrived. He was definitely good-looking, with dark hair and eyes and a disarming smile. Mama and I exchanged approving glances over his shoulder as he bent over the malfunctioning pancake. When the nurse joined us in our furtive assessment, I almost laughed aloud.

His looks were not his only asset, however; he was friendly and gentle and understanding. So understanding, in fact, that had he not been so obviously *male*, I would have sworn he had experienced a mastectomy! "*What is this?*" I thought. "*A psychiatrist in disguise?*" Nevertheless, I appreciated his concern. He cut and sealed a tube that he suspected was causing the trouble and then recompressed the pancake. He, too, assured me that I would feel better tomorrow.

When he had gone, the nurse who had been assisting him remained to clean up. "Wow!" I said.

She laughed understandingly. "You've got to stand in line," she said. "Every woman in this place cranes her neck when *he* walks by!" She continued, "And he's a good doctor, too. I've never heard a complaint from one of his patients."

"Well, I'm sure not going to be the first," I stated with conviction. Mama put on a "disapproving mother" face and said severely, "It's a good thing I'm here to keep an eye on you!"

"Yeah, Mama," I teased. "I saw you. Maybe I need to keep my eye on you!"

*   *   *

I lay as still as possible from one "interruption" to the next. I couldn't read or watch TV because of my headache. I couldn't eat because of the nausea. I couldn't rest because of the frequent hot and cold flashes. I didn't want to talk or think; I still longed for that long, drugged sleep, but now I would be willing to settle for a mere week-long hibernation rather than death. *I must be improving*, I thought. *I'm not real excited about living yet, but at least I don't want to die.*

The only thing that *didn't* bother me was my current incision; there was some discomfort, but it seemed minor compared to all my other complaints.

Dr. Connell came by again as promised, but she still had no solutions. "You've lost a lot of blood, but that's not serious; the urinalysis was okay; your incision is healing nicely. I don't know why you're running a fever. Let's wait and see how you are tomorrow." After talking to Mama a few minutes, she left.

With a great deal of self-control I refrained from screaming in my frustration, "Tomorrow . . . *tomorrow*! What about now? I'm so miserable and tired and sick. I just can't believe I have to feel this bad in a *hospital!*"

But evidently I did, because the night brought no relief whatsoever. Each time I had to get up I'd return to my bed practically convulsed from chills and weakness. Mama would pile covers on me and warm my face and hands with a washcloth wrung out in hot water. In just a short time I would break out in a sweat, throw off all the covers, and vomit. Then she would get a *cold* cloth to wipe my face and arms. Needless to say, I avoided frequent trips to the bathroom!

Around midnight I rang the buzzer and asked for something for pain; my incision had evidently decided that it might as well get in on the act and had challenged my headache to a contest. I was tired of tossing and turning and wrestling with covers, and I was concerned because Mama was not resting. When the nurse said she'd come in a few minutes, I thanked her and settled back to wait, confident that she *would*, as usual, be here soon. When thirty minutes had passed without a sign of her, I just assumed an emergency had arisen; I was squirming with discomfort but decided to be patient. When an hour had passed, I gave up the martyr act and rang the buzzer again.

Three hours later I still had not received anything for pain. I didn't fully understand what had happened, but somehow the key to the narcotics cabinet had been misplaced. All of us poor unfortunates who requested medication during those hours were informed, eventually, of the problem; however, that didn't relieve our pain. It was a long, long night. Mama and I both were fighting tears when the nurse finally appeared with my injection.

*　　*　　*

When Dr. Connell made rounds Friday morning, I stated in no uncertain terms that I'd had enough. "You have got to do *something*. I can't take any more." She was sympathetic and agreed that, whatever the undisclosed cause of my difficulties, I couldn't continue this way indefinitely. She ordered two huge injections of iron and started me on vitamins with iron. She ordered antibiotics and Darvon with aspirin, to be administered every four hours around the clock. And she changed my pain medicine again. "I hope all this helps," she said earnestly.

It did. Friday evening I ate my supper and—wonder of wonders—it stayed down! My headache was eased by the Darvon, my fever controlled by the aspirin, my elusive infection attacked by the antibiotic, and my blood boosted by the iron and vitamins. And most wonderful of all, the occasional pain shots I received *worked*!

A full tummy and freedom from pain did wonders for my spirits. Suddenly life had possibilities again. *I'm going to make it after all*! I thought gratefully. *And I'm glad!*

Chapter Sixteen

Doctors who do preventive—or prophylactic—breast surgery report that for those patients who accept the operation, it often gives them great peace of mind. Until the surgery many of these women fretted for weeks before each breast examination and lived with a constant fear of developing breast cancer.

You Can Fight Cancer and Win
Jane E. Brody

I have learned from experience that today is the day to live life to the fullest. Today is the day to be thankful for life and health and strength. Today is the day to appreciate loved ones and friends.

Life has a way of slipping in the unexpected. . . . And the unexpected may be shocking and heartbreaking. It is at such times and in such circumstances that we realize our human limitations, and we reach out to the Source of all strength and help, who is able to sustain and undergird in times of need. It is at such time that there is no doubt as to who is the Potter and who is the clay.

Bernice Nethery
The Sabine County *Reporter*

Weeping may endure for a night,
but joy cometh in the morning.
Psalm 30:5

Squeals of delight greeted the announcement that today was the day we put up the Advent calendar that would mark the days till Christmas; eager little hands grabbed for bright ornaments to hang on the red and green felt wall hanging.

"No, wait!" I said, lifting the box out of their reach. "We'll put *one* on today and *one* tomorrow. Every day when you get up, we'll put on *one* ornament. When the box is empty, Santa Claus will come!"

One pair of brown eyes and one pair of blue ones opened wide with wonder and excitement. I remembered the same expressions from Ross and Laura when they were this age. I had made a "countdown clock" for them from a paper plate attached to a wrapping paper covered box. Their photos and cutouts from old Christmas cards decorated it, and two dates—Ross's birthday on the nineteenth and Christmas on the twenty-fifth—were circled in red. The holiday season really began each year when that clock was put on the wall.

This calendar was more elaborate; I had been making the tiny felt ornaments for weeks, working every spare moment. Rick and Lana had been fascinated with the whole process and would sit for long periods of time, watching me sew on sequins and trim and then stuff little felt cutouts. Lana, wide-eyed, watched me make the first one, unaware of what I was doing. When I showed her the finished product, a little blue elephant with sequined ears, she looked at it with awe. With an unaccustomed gentleness she cradled it in her two hands. "Did you make it for *me*, Mommy? A little 'epamunt' for *me*?"

I tried to resist, but her obvious joy in my creation made it impossible. I gave her the "epamunt" and made another for my project; she carried that tiny decoration around with her everywhere she went for days, even to bed.

I sat down on the stairs and watched the children play with the little characters for a few minutes before putting them up again. *December 1 seemed a long way off when I started work on these things*, I mused, scarcely able to believe so much time had elapsed. *I made the first one soon after my last surgery, and that's been two months ago!*

My thoughts drifted back in time, and I recalled briefly some of the events of the past months. . . .

My convalescence had been slow; somehow my body just didn't "snap back" the way it had before. I was weak, easily fatigued, and continued to have low-grade fever almost daily. Another physical problem plagued me for months following surgery: my "thermostat" was upset, and I was alternately freezing cold or burning up. My arm, however, did not require nearly as much therapy as the other one had; the difference was that the large chest muscles were not removed.

My lovely, loving family continued to support me in every way. During the early weeks of my recuperation, Bernice prepared innumerable meals and gave her time and love unstintingly. Jan kept Rick and Lana for days at a time; her husband, Jim, always welcomed them and never seemed to mind the frequent additions to his household. Words of encouragement, prayers on my behalf, and numerous expressions of love from other family members and friends helped speed my recovery.

My mental outlook had climbed steadily since I had "hit bottom" in the hospital. The relief I felt since my prophylactic mastectomy was inexpressible; I never regretted having the surgery. I no longer dreaded monthly breast-check time, nor did I live with the fear of breast cancer recurring. True to my presurgery prediction, I *did* feel more normal with no breasts than with one. And when I purchased my second prosthesis, I felt almost as good as new. To make it even better, the pharmacy had expanded its line to carry a soft, smooth-cupped bra, similar to what I had always worn. Now I could wear my knits again!

Several things had occurred that upset me during my recovery time. Anita's baby had been born without abdominal muscles and with underdeveloped lungs; he had a fragile hold on life for a few weeks and still faces an uncertain future. Two weeks later Joanna's little boy was born prematurely and was kept in the incubator for quite a while; I had shared Joanna's uncertainty about his prognosis and her agony in not getting to hold her baby for over a week.

Then, too, Mama's ordeal was constantly on my mind. She had started her chemotherapy treatments, and they were making her very sick. I felt so helpless and heartsick at seeing her in such distress; however, she rarely complained and was determined to continue her life in a normal manner. Somehow, knowing her cancer was inoperable, and, therefore, still there *inside* her, was almost impossible for me to bear. Yet, I knew lymphoma was one of the most easily treated cancers; new drugs were proving very successful in controlling the disease.

In spite of problems that troubled both me and these people I loved so dearly, I continued to progress physically, mentally, and spiritually. On October 10 I made the following entry in my journal:

> All in all, I feel closer to God than I ever have. I feel His presence, His guiding hand, His assurance that all is well even though by human standards and worldly guidelines, things have never been worse for us.
>
> It has to be the "peace that passeth understanding." I am so thankful for it.

The days had been full with school activities, football games, and Christmas planning. And late in November, Ross's seventh grade basketball team began their games. He was a starter, and I was proud of him. We went to all his games and thoroughly enjoyed them. (Basketball was always a favorite sport of mine anyway; I had jokingly commented many times that the only reason I went to high school was to play basketball!)

Thanksgiving had been a wonderful holiday this year. Mama and I were both unusually thankful for life itself, something we had almost taken for granted before. Having our entire family together for dinner on Thanksgiving Day was a special blessing. My dining room table was expanded to serve all fifteen of us, and it was loaded with a huge assortment of good food. I had baked mince and pecan pies, made the dressing and giblet gravy, baked the ham and turkey, and made Ross's favorite crescent rolls. Others had contributed salads, vegetables, a pork roast, fruit cake, various candies, and cranberry sauce. It was all delicious!

Two other events had combined to make Thanksgiving Day "extra special": the Nethery bunch, all twenty of them, shared dessert and coffee at our house that evening, and the Aggies beat

Texas in the annual Turkey Day football game! (Jim, Ken, and Pat's husband, Tom, are all Texas A&M alumni!)

The days from Thanksgiving on were full. I was busy "helping Santa" make doll clothes, and I was making most all my Christmas gifts. Decorating egg shells with rice paper napkins for my yearly addition to our collection of homemade ornaments had been another big project. I was planning for, and looking eagerly forward to, the *very best Christmas ever*!

*　　*　　*

My thoughts were interrupted by Lana's shrill voice. "Mommy, Rick won't *share* with me!" I looked down to find Lana sitting with a lap full of ornaments and Rick holding one in each hand! Carefully, I retrieved them and placed all but one in the box.

"Rick, will you put this little Christmas tree on the calendar?" Then quickly, before Lana had time for a protest, I continued, "Lana, tomorrow *you* can put up the little blue 'epamunt!' "

I gathered them close to me, and we sat in silence looking at the brightly colored wall hanging with its one small decoration—the Christmas tree. Christmas still looked a long way off.

*　　*　　*

Days followed happy days, each one filled to the brim with holiday preparations, activities, and expectations. So many events marked this joyous season that it seemed impossible, looking back from the vantage point of the New Year, that we had actually done all that in so short a time!

Ross's glorious red-white-and-blue thirteenth birthday, our last bicentennial celebration of the year, was an exciting day. Mama, Bernice, and I had hosted a buffet supper in our home for the school administrators and Jim's office workers and their spouses. The church progressive dinner ended up here for dessert and Christmas carol singing. And Greg and Amy spent the week prior to the twenty-fifth with us; we filled the days with fun: baking Christmas cookies, eating peanuts in front of the fire, having nightly read-aloud sessions, trekking through the woods, Christmas caroling around the community (we all rode in the back of the pickup), dressing the big white rooster we'd been fattening for Christmas dinner, shooting fireworks, enjoying frequent holiday visitors, and doing last-minute Christmas shopping.

Christmas Eve at the Netherys and Christmas Day at the Millses were both wonderful family get-togethers. Christmas night I had ended my journal entry in this manner:

> This was the most wonderful Christmas I remember. The whole season was great. I tried very hard to make it extra special for all of us this year.
>
> Life is so precious.
>
> Thank You, God, for Your Son, for Christmas, for life, and love, and family.

Two days later, December 27, I recorded a slight change of mood and an unusual (and disturbing) dream I had:

> We took down the tree and other decorations. We all hated to see it come down; it was the most perfect tree I've ever seen. We'll *never* find one that pretty again!
>
> I've been in a bad mood all day. Christmas "let-down" maybe. I'm also worried about my left hand—it continues to hurt and there is some swelling. What if it's the cancer spreading? It scares me.
>
> I dreamed last night that a great big man, a sea captain, came here claiming I was his, and I had to go with him. He was very nice—I liked and trusted him—but I was dismayed

220

because I didn't want to leave my home. The captain said I knew him, and Jim and the kids said I knew him, but I insisted he was a stranger and I'd never seen him before.

I begged Jim to do something. He said he would, and he called the police and the lawyers. None of them could do anything—the captain had "the proper papers" needed to claim me.

He promised me a beautiful home, unlimited travel, and everything my heart desired. I would have gladly gone except for Jim and the kids.

I woke myself up before he could take me away. What a strange dream! What does it mean? Anything? Nothing? Was the captain *death*?

It was days before I could put that dream out of my mind. Normally I don't remember dreams, nor am I one to put much stock in dream interpretations. I can't explain why this one affected me so.

$$* \quad * \quad *$$

Ross and Laura went to Jeannie's to spend the week after Christmas; Jim and I enjoyed the "little kids" and the long, quiet nights we spent together after Rick and Lana were in bed. We celebrated New Year's Eve sitting quietly in front of the fire listening to records. The next day we went to Diboll to have dinner with the Weavers and to get Ross and Laura.

We all joked about the blackeyed peas which were a necessity for a "proper" New Year's Day dinner. According to old Southern custom, you *must* eat blackeyed peas and hog jowl to be "lucky" the following year. Although none of us believed the superstition, we concluded that we must not have eaten enough peas *last* New Year's Day—1976 was definitely not the best year for any of us!

*   *   *

Early in January I went back to Dr. Garrett for my monthly checkup and took Laura with me. We were concerned about some lumps that had appeared in her neck. Although she had had *one* since babyhood, others had come in the past few months. In view of all the disastrous lumps Mama and I had experienced lately, we were all worried—especially Laura. Dr. Garrett checked us both thoroughly. I was pronounced "good for another month" and the problem with my hand turned out to be just "edema," swelling that sometimes accompanies a radical mastectomy, especially if the surgery is followed with radiation. Dr. Garrett prescribed a diuretic tablet for me to take several times a week.

He discovered lumps in both sides of Laura's neck and in her armpits. Her tonsils were also enlarged. He sent us to the lab for blood tests so that we could rule out mononucleosis. Several days later I called his office for the results. Her blood was fine! Dr. Garrett counseled waiting. "Since she feels good and the blood tests were fine, I think it's probably nothing to be concerned about. I wouldn't recommend any further tests right now."

I reassured Laura and seemed to ease her fears, but I continued to be uneasy. Later I took her to Dr. McCall, a pediatrician in Lufkin, and he gave approximately the same advice. After having another blood test done, a chest X-ray taken, and a TB test "stamped" on her arm, there was nothing else to do but trust the doctors and pray that their advice was correct. But she was only ten—so young to be having problems of this nature already.

I probably would have been perfectly satisfied with their advice if cancer had not entered our lives twice in recent months. *Will I always have this fear with me now?* I wondered. *Every time a problem arises will my first reaction be to wonder if it's cancer again?* Somehow, *before* cancer strikes, you never really believe it will happen to you. Then once it has, you have no difficulty believing it can and will happen again.

*   *   *

The early months of 1977 found me "back to normal." I was able to do anything I had done "before" and was feeling just great. My monthly visits to Dr. Garrett were proving to be just routine, although each month I seemed to come up with some minor ailment to report.

Once my arm and hand swelled so much that I had to take fluid pills daily and keep my arm above my head for several days. After that, I rarely had trouble with swelling though I was never again able to wear my beautiful wedding band, and my upper arm remained slightly larger than my normal right one.

Another time I developed heart "flutters" which turned out to be a side effect of the fluid pills. I stopped taking them, and my heart trouble (which I was *sure* was cancer of the heart!) vanished.

One month I reported a tiny bump on the inside of my little finger on the left hand. That "cancer," too, disappeared.

In January I had bruised my leg, and the place stayed "discolored" for several months. I was sure this was an example of one of the seven warning signals of cancer—a sore that does not heal—but Dr. Garrett assured me it was nothing.

I began reading everything I could on the subject of breast cancer. I wanted to know *everything*, good and bad. I wanted to know just what my chances for survival were, what kinds of symptoms heralded possible metastasis, and what kinds of follow-up procedures were most widely recommended. I also wanted to know if I'd been treated in the most widely accepted and proven way. Any time I had a question, or even a doubt about why I was treated in "such-and-such" a way, Dr. Garrett patiently explained what I wanted to know. I became firmly convinced that the radical mastectomy and the cobalt treatments were right *for me* and had given me the best possible chance of living out my normal life span. I also learned that what was right for another breast cancer victim might not be right for me; each case is different and should be treated individually.

*   *   *

In late March, Mama received some excellent news. Dr. Kistler told us that she was in remission! Much rejoicing and thanksgiving accompanied his announcement that there was no active cancer and that she would not have to have any more treatments for a while. How thankful we all were for those horrible chemotherapy treatments! How thankful we were for the knowledge of her skilled and concerned doctors! How glad we were that she had not discontinued the treatments when they were making her so miserable!

Mama had never feared death; she looked it squarely in the face and saw a friend. But, given a reprieve through remission, she looked forward passionately to a summer without treatments and the health to enjoy her grandchildren, to picnic at the lake, and to work in her garden.

I looked forward to summer for another reason—it signified the end of the first year after cancer invaded my body. For some reason, I believed that if I could make it through that first year without a recurrence, I'd "have it made." As the end of the year approached, I grew uneasy. My left leg had begun to bother me with weakness, an aching in the thigh, and a slight swelling on the top of the leg a few inches above the knee. In addition to that, I was beginning to feel tired again, and the anxiety of the ailing leg (bone cancer, surely!) combined with the fatigue to add up to *worry*.

When I went for my regular monthly checkup at the end of April, I expressed my concern to Dr. Garrett. I reminded him that Dr. Kistler had told me when I was taking the cobalt treatments that at the end of the first year I would need to have some X-rays taken and some scans and other tests done. Dr. Garrett, sensing how concerned I was and how eager I was to get this first year's checkup behind me, suggested that I check into the hospital for the tests. Gratefully I accepted his proposal. I was ready to join the "land of the living" again, and I just didn't think I could do it until I got that "all clear" report after Year One.

Sunday, May 1, 1977, I checked into Memorial Hospital for tests.

Chapter Seventeen

My personal experiences with cancer made a tremendous impact on me and how I conduct my life. I might have responded with fear, avoidance, ignorance, and a sense of inevitability. I might have said, "Cancer runs in my family. I'm sure to get it. So why not just accept my fate?" But I realized that fear is cancer's greatest ally. Fear blocks the acquisition of life-saving knowledge. Fear keeps people from adopting sensible living habits, getting periodic checkups, recognizing and acting upon early suspicious symptoms—taking the very steps that can make the difference between winning and losing the battle against cancer.

You Can Fight Cancer and Win
Jane Brody

I am an old man and have known a great many troubles, but most of them have never happened.
Mark Twain

Rejoice everymore.
Pray without ceasing.
In everything give thanks:
for this is the will of God in Christ Jesus concerning you.

1 Thessalonians 5:16-18

The room was so clean and cool and quiet; I lay back grate-fully on the bed. I was tired from the efforts of trying to get the children, the house, and myself ready for another hospital stay. I kept reminding myself that this was just for a couple of days, and that it was just for routine tests. Yet I was restless and apprehensive.

I had brought my journal with me this time; I was enter-taining the idea of attempting an article—possibly even a book—about my experiences with breast cancer, and I thought I might have time between tests to get some thoughts together. Bernice had provided the stimulus to the germ of an idea I had secretly been harboring when she asked an unexpected question: "Why don't you write a book about breast cancer?"

My initial reaction had been, "I can't write a book!" Yet I *did* enjoy writing and I *did* have a testimony to share that might be helpful to others. The possibility that I had a talent and a testimony that might combine to bring glory to God's name thrilled me beyond words. *Why not try?* I asked myself, reasonably enough. *If God is in this, it will accomplish His will and purpose. If He is leading, I can do it. If not, it will have been an exercise of faith and good intentions.*

I had thought of the phrase "sacrifice of thanksgiving" and had looked it up in the Psalms. (For truly, if I should attempt a project of such magnitude as writing a book, it would involve a sacrifice, not just on my part, but from the whole family.) I had read from my Bible: "Oh that men would praise the Lord for his goodness, and for his wonderful works to the children of men! And let them sacrifice the *sacrifices of thanksgiving*, and declare his works with rejoicing" (Ps. 107:21, 22).

Could I make the "sacrifice?" How I'd love to "declare his wonderful works" to *me* with rejoicing! *We'll see*, I thought. *We'll see what this week brings first.*

I picked up my journal, glanced back over the past few pages, and read an entry I had made on Sunday, April 24:

I had to play the organ in Aunt B.'s absence today, and my left leg surely did get tired. I'm a little anxious about it. My legs have always been strong. They should be—I've always exercised a lot (bike riding each day in Diboll and walking three miles a day here). Why, then, the weakness in the left one?

Obviously, I'm afraid it's cancer. I guess when the "impossible" happens once, you always fear it again. I should go on and have it checked immediately, I guess, but it's probably nothing.

I had my hand X-rayed a few months ago when it first started hurting—nothing showed up, but soon the swelling started which has bothered me off and on since. I guess the pain was the prelude to the swelling—it doesn't hurt now. But I felt silly for getting the X-ray!

Also, I've complained to Dr. Garrett for months now of heart palpitations. Later I read in a newspaper that the fluid pills I was taking sometimes cause that side effect. I quit taking them and the "lurching heart" quit, too. So again I was upset for nothing.

I know it is stupid to think every little problem is metastasis of the breast cancer. I hope as more time passes I'll get over doing that.

And on Wednesday, April 27, I wrote:

I'm feeling a little better—my leg still bothers me, though. I'm really eager (anxious?) to get it X-rayed. I'm shortwinded and weak. I have to struggle to make my walk every day.

Of course, it's possible all of this is in my *head*! I'll admit I *look* for trouble, possibly because I know too many facts. Cancer is now thought to be a chronic disease; it can recur. And if it does it usually happens the first year. I don't want to *die* because I failed to notice a symptom. Now *that* would be stupid.

Later on that same day I had made an entry of a completely different nature:

Noon: I was just feeding Emily her bottle and had put a Leonard Bernstein record on for a quiet time. [Emily was a darling little six-month-old baby I had been keeping daily since February so that her mother, who couldn't find a "regular" sitter, could continue teaching. I was home with two anyway; one more didn't make much difference, and I could certainly use the money!]

Lana was lying on the floor watching me feeding the baby. When Tchaikovsky's "Spanish Dance" began playing, she stood up and said, "That music teaches me how to dance!" And she started twirling and spinning around the room, beautifully "in step" with what she was hearing!

I watched, fascinated. At one point she even fell dramatically to the floor, writhing and twisting to the music. She was beautiful! Tears came to my eyes as I thought of the great privilege I had of watching such innocent beauty being moved by the music.

I can't express what I felt. I know I prayed silently, *O God!*
Look! Share this with me. This perfect little creation of Yours
dancing with such grace and beauty. Look what You've created!
Enjoy Your creations—the child and the music.

This is my gift to You today, God. Turn Your weary eyes from
the evils and the wickedness of this world and feast them on the
perfection of this moment.

Thank You, God! Oh, thank You for this glimpse of heaven—
the hope of a new world to share with You, full of beauty, love,
innocence, and praise.

I smiled to myself as I read the entry immediately following
that one:

Rick came in a few minutes ago bringing a snail he'd found
to show me. However, he dropped it on the carpet before he
reached the kitchen. *"Find* that snail," I commanded. After
looking for several minutes he stood up, shrugged his little
shoulders and said, "I guess he just *snailed* on outa here,
Mom!"

My eyes filled with tears as I thought of the four children.
They were all such joys to us—so precious and beautiful. *They*
need me, God, I prayed defiantly. *I have to be there for them.* I
struggled to control my thoughts before they dissolved into
tears. Picking up my pen I wrote in my journal:

I am here at Memorial Hospital. It's kind of nice to be
sitting here watching T.V. and knowing I haven't a *thing* to
do!

Jim brought me up here this afternoon. We took Lana to
Linda's. She was happy to stay. Rick is at Mama's right now.

Tomorrow Dr. G. has scheduled a chest X-ray, routine lab
work, a brain scan, a bone survey, and a liver scan. Sounds
like a busy day.

I'm back in my old room—218—on Henderson. It's good to
see the nurses here again. They are all so nice.

I think I'll take a long hot bath and turn in!

Before I went to sleep I shared my fears and longings with
God: *You know my thoughts, Father, even better than I do.
You know I fear a recurrence of cancer. You know I feel that I
will die from it.*

*But Father, please give me this summer! Let me have these
three months to be with my family. Give me enough time to write
my book. I've done so little for You! Give me a chance now to
share the reality of Your great love and constant care with others
who need You as much as I have.*

My fears of imminent death may have been perfectly groundless; God may have already planned for me to live a full, long
life. However, I was compelled to pray in this way; I merely
expressed the deepest feelings of my soul. And God heard me,
calmed my fears, and comforted me with His presence.

* * *

The next two days were full of tests. In addition to those
ordered by Dr. Garrett, Dr. Connell did a pelvic examination
and took a Pap smear. I hardly ever left my room, except to go to
the radiation center. I had very few visitors because I had requested that no one come. I just wanted to "hide" and rest for a
few days; I didn't feel like making conversation or seeing anyone.

Dr. Garrett came in Monday evening and told me the results of
some of my tests. All of them were good, and nothing had showed
up on the X-ray of my leg! Relieved, but frustrated, I asked,
"Well, what is it then? It can't be my imagination. You can feel it.
Dr. Connell can feel it. I can feel it."

He shrugged and examined the "lump" again. "I don't know, but it's *not* cancer. Maybe it's an old bruise or a muscle strain. Don't worry about it."

I hated that phrase. I *did* worry about it! But I compromised. "Okay, Dr. Garrett. If everything else checks out okay, and you tell me I'm 'cancer free' when you release me this time, I promise I'll quit worrying. I've been telling myself that if I made it through this year I was going to *live*; that target date is almost here and *I will not worry any more after that*."

May 3, 1977

It is Tuesday afternoon, 5:30. Dr. Garrett came in a few minutes ago and told me that all my tests were clear! I still can't believe it; yet I am so thankful.

Evidently a lot of my physical problems were caused by emotional ones. Having been through three surgeries in less than a year, facing the trauma of Mama's cancer, and experiencing the emotional *murder* of knowing I had cancer was just too much for me.

Where there had been no serious problems before, now there were many. "What happened once can happen again," I reasoned. Consequently, I had begun anticipating—even imagining—new ills. ("Making mountains out of molehills," so to speak!)

Rebelliously, I refused to accept even short term limitations; I tried to be "Super Woman"—out to prove to myself and the world that I was still me and still capable of doing all the things I've always done. And *more*.

In addition to normal "cancer fears" and the temporary decreased physical strength was the "female factor." Realizing fully how *blessed* I am in every way—even just to be alive—still sometimes I feel sorry for myself. I wish I still had my breasts. I feel unattractive. Sometimes I think, "What would I do if something happened to Jim? Who would *have* me?" And I think, when some man gives me an interested look: "He wouldn't look at me that way if he *knew*."

I know those things are stupid; yet they are real, female feelings. And I *am* still a woman.

I had a long discussion with Dr. Garrett today after he assured me that all my tests were fine (brain scan, liver/spleen scan, blood tests, gall bladder, upper G.I., skull X-rays, etc.).

His opinion was that I needed to pace myself—quit overdoing it. And quit worrying about *cancer*. "I've cured you of cancer," he stated flatly. "And you don't have to prove *anything* to *anybody!*"

But how do I quit being *me?* How do I learn to let things go? And yet, if the alternative is *this* (working myself into an illness and being tired and tense), *do I have a choice?*

Evidently I need to re-evaluate my whole life; yet being a homemaker *is* my life. It's what God called me to do. That hasn't changed. Now where do I go from there?

I put down my pen and tried to think it all out. I quickly came up with one very important and obvious fact: *God didn't call me to be a housekeeper. He called me to be a homemaker. There's a world of difference. (I've known this all along, of course, but sometimes it's hard to remember.) Previously, I've been able to do both with ease; now—hopefully only temporarily—I can't. So, in view of what Dr. Garrett has told me, I've got to let something "slide" a little—obviously, the house.*

I also must realize that I don't have to prove anything to anyone, and if I can't keep a spotless house, it's no criminal offense. Being a good wife and mother is the most important part of my job. (However, being honest with myself, I have to admit that I don't think I've "shortchanged" my family too often.) Each day is a gift from God; each hour with Jim and the kids a treasure. I will try harder to realize that.

One other thing came to mind: *I need to take care of myself—pamper myself a little more and realize I need just like the other family members need. God has given me abilities, creative urgings, a testimony to share, talents to develop, a special personality. He thinks I'm important as a person; He wants to care for me and help me develop to my full potential just as I want to do for my children!*

My thoughts shifted and the enormity of what Dr. Garrett had told me earlier dawned on me. *I am okay! There is no evidence of cancer anywhere in my body! All of my fears were groundless!*

I thought happily of the long summer that stretched ahead—sunny days of swimming (in my beautiful, new, specially ordered swimsuit!) and picnicking and enjoying the kids. Vacation time meant skiing expeditions, canning and freezing, and roasting weiners in the back yard! All the pleasant, enjoyable summertime things I'd missed last year rose ahead of me invitingly.

I bowed my head in a prayer of thanksgiving: *Thank You, Father, for the good news. Please help me now in my resolve not to worry any more. Help me learn to live "one day at a time" and never, never take the gift of life for granted. Thank You, God, oh, thank You!*

I lifted my head and set my face determinedly toward "tomorrow," my spirit renewed and my heart freshly washed by the cleansing tears of gratitude and praise.

My joy was full. God had given me a reprieve. It was now "one year and counting," and from now on I planned to make each moment count!

Postscript

The expected telephone call from Susan came last Monday evening, May 15, and my heart was lifted in joy and thanksgiving as she calmly and pleasantly told me that after a thorough physical examination Dr. Garrett had said: "I find no signs of recurrence of cancer or metastasis."

It has been exactly two years since the words *cancer* and *mastectomy* became grim realities in our immediate family. Before that I had assumed malignacies could happen to others or to older people but not to beautiful, radiant, fun-loving Susan. A wonderful wife, a devoted mother, an ideal daughter-in-law, an inspiring Christian, she was too young and too full of the joy of living to be stricken with such a subtle, treacherous disease.

The doctor's shocking words to us gathered in that small waiting room at Memorial Hospital, Lufkin, when Susan went in for surgery two years ago left us stunned and helpless. She did have cancer; he felt he should do a radical mastectomy. We waited silently and prayerfully for what seemed like an eternity. Then, almost in a daze, we went to her room after she was brought from recovery. One by one we went to her bedside and looked at that precious one lying there swathed in bandages, her eyes deep wells of hurt and sorrow, sorrow not just for herself but for those of us who loved her. Words seemed futile. We gently touched her and kissed her pale, cold cheeks, and she knew that whatever happened she was completely immersed in love and undergirded with prayer.

Time moved on, and we were forced to accept reality and to meet the problems of each day. We all found extra strength for extra times of need just as Susan did. We found that our God is, indeed, master of every circumstance—that in dark hours He is still the source of peace, joy, and love.

Days turned into weeks, weeks into months, and we saw Susan courageously "reaching for recovery." Once again the tantalizing aroma of homemade bread and rolls began to come from her kitchen. The Netherys' beautiful hill began to echo with the sweet sounds of laughter and fellowship as relatives and friends began to gather there, share the warm hospitality of their home, and rejoice in Susan's return to good health.

Recently, I have seen Susan strikingly dressed in Oriental style, serving Chinese food at a Tasting Tea. This is an annual affair sponsored by the Young Women's Christian League, a community service organization in which Susan is active. I have seen her judging events at our school's Field Day and on the evening of the same day serving barbecue to hungry athletes at the Athletic Barbecue. I have seen her playing the piano in church and teaching a Sunday school class. I have seen her picking berries, jogging through the woods along her favorite trail, and serving delicious outdoor meals or picnic lunches to family and friends.

I have seen this family go through two trying years without any family relationships breaking down. In fact, each person has become more aware that every day is a special day, that each member is important to the other, and that trials can be a means of growth and maturity. Out of the experiences of the past two years something beautiful has emerged which should give hope to all who face any kind of crisis: a young mother and wife went through a traumatic experience, and a family faced many difficulties and adjustments, but through love and faith, courage and determination, cooperation and dedication, that family has moved into a realm of unity and purpose which is rarely seen today.

As this book goes to press, Susan is as beautiful, gracious, poised, and radiant as she was before undergoing two mastectomies. Perhaps there are scars, but they are covered with a new sensitivity and deeper appreciation for life and beauty.

Bernice Nethery
May 18, 1978